HUNGRY HORSES

*The true story of two horses with courage,
stamina and the will to live, and how they helped
shape the history of the Hungry Horse Canyon area*

For order information call
1-406-387-5033
Or Write;
Judy Rabidue
Box 260328
Martin City Mt. 59926

Library of Congress Pre-Assigned Card Number
2002116666

Printed and bound in China
First Printing • **ISBN # 1-930043-27-9**

This book is dedicated to Tex and Jerry:

Two very brave horses who's story of bravery and survival against the harsh and cruel elements of winter in a Montana wilderness brought about the history of the Hungry Horse Canyon area. May they long be remembered for their gallant efforts against the odds.

Thanks for not giving up boys.

CONTENTS

INTRODUCTION

This is the story of a team of two work horses that became famous by almost starving to death.

I was first introduced to Tex and Jerry when I was about four years old. My parents stopped at the art studio and store of Blake the Wood Carver. I remember while Mr. Blake was showing my folks all his beautiful wood carvings, I was drawn straight to a carving of a very skinny horse. I pulled on my mother's sleeve and asked, "Why is this horse so skinny, and he looks so sad. Why don't they fix him." Mr. Blake came to the rescue of my mother and proceeded to tell us the short story of how two work horses had gotten lost. When they were found they looked just like the statue. He assured me that in real life they had been rescued and lived to a ripe old age. That only set me off into a barrage of questions about the horses. Because I was only four, I was shut down rather quickly by the adults for my annoying babbling.

Over my lifetime those two horses haunted me and I could never quite get them out of my mind. I felt that they deserved to be recognized and given some credit for what they had gone through, and that because of their ordeal, a name came to life. The name Hungry Horse was born and used from then until today.

In 1980 I was attending college at Flathead Valley Community College. I was in the library doing research on a paper that I was writing when I had a Tex and Jerry attack and wondered if just maybe I could find out a little something about them. That sort of started me on my quest to write this book. I could only find one clipping from a Spokane paper about them. Well, needless to say, I had to get back to school and take care of business.

Then in 1996, the wonderful newspaper called The Hungry Horse News ran an old article that had been originally published in their paper in 1946. I was thrilled; the article gave me enough information about the horses to set my imagination flying. I hope you enjoy my thoughts on how their lives might have been, as much as I have enjoyed bringing them back to life.

I need to thank my husband, Ron, for his wonderful gentle prodding to get me to finish this book. I also need to thank my dear friend, Carol Walters, for sitting with me for hours going through the book and making sure it was written in a way you would all enjoy reading. Her help was the most valuable tool I had. I also need to give a special thanks to my mom and dad for moving all of us here to the Flathead, a most magical place to live. My darling mom is also a sharp stick to get me going on writing and finishing this book. My family has been a wonderful support and a great sounding board. I also want to thank Gary Crowe for his help in proof reading and Scott Publishing and their crew who have made a special effort to make this book a reality.

The story is part fact and part how I thought it might have been, but the photo and history section is completely factual.

1946 — Hungry Horse News — 1996

Hungry Horse

Memorable name began with two horses lost for a month in the snowy South Fork

Choosing the right name for his newspaper was one of Mel Ruder's finest—and easiest—decisions.

"I wanted an area name and didn't want to use Columbia Falls," Ruder said. "I knew this paper had to be out and not just in Columbia Falls and I knew Hungry Horse Dam was coming."

"The name Hungry Horse was western and would tie the area together," he added.

And so the *Hungry Horse News* was born.

The name "hungry horse" already was on a creek, lake, mountain and town. Ruder reported the story of the hungry horse name in one of his first editions. November 28, 1946

The hungry horse story

During the winter of 1900 and 1901, William Prindiville was freighting from Belton up the North Fork to Kintla Lake where oil was supposed to be. They were taking up the drill, casings and pipe so when they struck oil, they could pipe it down the railroad.

The supplies and horses were shipped from Columbia Falls to

> **"**They were nothing but skin and bones and you have never seen two hungrier horses than they were.**"**
>
> —Bill Prindiville

Belton (now West Glacier) on a train. After the job was finished they headed back to Columbia Falls on the road since they had no load.

The men took the harness off the team leaders and chained them to the back of their sleighs.

After crossing the South Fork of the Flathead River, they discovered the Prindiville's two lead horses—Tex and Jerry— were missing.

"They must have looked for a better place to ford because it was all ice and slippery," Prindiville wrote later. "Instead of trying to cross there, they went up the South Fork for a better ford or bridge."

They were missing for a month in belly-deep snow and Prindiville couldn't find them or their tracks.

When he finally found them, they had been living on willows

and brush. Prindiville had to break a trail and pack in oats before he could get them to stand the trip out.

"They were nothing but skin and bones and you have never seen two hungrier horses than they were," Bill recalled. It took him two days to bring them home.

As he went through Columbia Falls with Tex and Jerry, people came out to look at the bony survivors. They knew he'd been looking for them for more than a month.

Told they were up the South Fork, an onlooker spoke up and said that was awful hungry horse country up there.

Jerry was later traded to Charlie Ruple and used to pull the Kalispell fire wagon. Tex was used by the Kalispell Mercantile Co. on a freight wagon.

Editor's note: David Prindiville, who wrote the account of the hungry horse, was the brother of Bill mentioned in the story. He and Bill were the first Montanans to attend Notre Dame University, then an academy, in 1880s.

1946 — Hungry Horse News — 1996

This was a thankful day for Tex, one of the original hungry horses. Grazing on green pasture, he is shown with white horse, Judy, on LaSalle farm of William Prindiville in the summer of 1900 or 1901.

Chapter 1:
Out of the Fire
and Into the Story

The barn door flew open with its usual loud and obnoxious bang. The ring of our handler's deep booming voice broke the delightful silence of the barn. Before I could finish blinking the sleep from my eyes and focus on the light shining in, I found myself on the usual route of exiting the warmth and comfort of my stall. When my eyes met the fullness of the daylight they were greeted with the cold grayness of a winter's morning. The clouds were so thick and heavy, that they blocked out the rays of struggling sun, trying so desperately to break through and make their mark on the day. The clouds ranged in colors from bright gray to a deep, dark black. They were hanging so low I felt like I could just reach up and touch them. I thought for a minute, what if... If only I could touch them, maybe I could break them up and chase them away. They were filled with a soaking dampness, the kind that penetrates my whole body. I always hate days like this... they make my poor old bones creak and crack and my muscles ache.

It was beginning to look like it would be a regular winter's workday just like many that had passed before it. Oh well... I need to get moving. I need to warm up these old muscles and limber up my joints, and get ready for the workday ahead, for I have a job to do.

The cold stiff harness squeaked in rebellion as the handler was adjusting it on my back and pulling it up tight on me for the last time. As it tightened it got buried into my thick winter's coat of hair and disappeared from sight. The handler backed me into position and hooked me up to the delivery wagon.

My early morning frump grew bigger at the sound of the always cheerful greeting, "Top of the morning to you, Tex." The chirping in my ear came from my team mate, Tipper... alias "Chipper Tipper." How can she be so happy on a morning like this? I thought. Tipper yawned and stretched and acted like she was delighted to go to work. Oh! I would love to be young like her, again.

The handler's loud cluck lets us know it is time to step out, and start our daily routine of delivering goods. The gray dull mist coming from our breath only added to the dullness of the day. My body creaked almost as loud as the harness and it certainly had as many miles on it as the old harness did... maybe more.

I don't know why, maybe it is the dullness and sharp coldness of the day, but my mind keeps filling with thoughts of the past and another very cold, gray, damp winter's day. Such thoughts make my body shiver and my eyes water. I have, for a moment, returned to the winter of 1900 and the terrible ordeal that my friend Jerry and I survived. As my mind wanders back, the rush of fear feels as real today as it was back then. I can only hold such thoughts for a second or two, for I must make my mind get back to the task at hand and deal with the up coming traffic.

My dreary thoughts of the past were abruptly interrupted by a loud shout of "TEX, TIPPER, whoa, whoa there now, whoa!" A sharp pain in my mouth accompanied the loud shouts. In a blink of a second Tipper and I found ourselves doing what we call in horse talk, the "wild horse two step," one of the most dreaded and feared situations there is in the horse world. This step evolves when us horses catch our bodies going one direction and our feet trying to go in another. At the same time we are trying desperately to maintain our footing. We must also hold back a heavy load behind us. The handler was bearing down on the bits in our mouths with as much force as he was pulling on the squealing hand brakes. Our mouths were stinging in pain and the skin felt like it was getting ripped off of our lips. The cold hard steel bits were bearing down and clanging on our teeth and jaws. It felt like our jawbones would give way and just break in a million pieces! We honestly thought he was going to rip the bits right out of our mouths. Oh how I wish he knew just how strong he was and what he was doing to us! The harness dug deep into the backs of our legs and tightened around our bellies so tight that it took our breath away. The pain from the harness was so intense and harsh it felt like it was cutting us from our back legs all the way up and out our front legs. It pinched and pulled our backs and caused us to groan in pain. Our feet were slipping and sliding in all directions; we felt totally out of control of the situation. We dug deep and hard and hoped with some help from our winter shoes with pegs in them, that we could get some traction and be able to stop. The fact of the matter is, when the streets are this snowy and icy it makes it almost impossible to stop, let alone hold a full wagon behind us. I am not sure exactly how we did it, but through the pain and fear, we managed to bring the wagon to a screeching halt, just short of the fire horses and wagons, speeding by the ends of our noses.

The combination of the screaming wagon brakes and the fire bells were so loud that we couldn't even hear our own hearts beating. I thought my heart was going to jump right out of my chest. I have had a lot of scares in my life but only one other time in my life had my heart ever beat this fast and hard. Instantly my heartbeats swept me back into 1900 and the fear I felt when I almost lost my friend Jerry.

As quickly as the thought came, it passed, and shifted back to the present and the thought of what might have happened if either of us had fallen. It became a thought almost too much to bear or to let myself think about.

I'm a seasoned work horse and have been through scary moments like this one, on other occasions. So... I took a deep breath and blew off all the fear and let go of the pain. I gathered myself up in the quickest way possible.

The stinging pain was enough to upset anyone, but of course I was not pulling with just anyone... It happened to be the young sassy horse Tipper. She was always worried about how she looked and how she performed her duties as a delivery horse. She had to have been in as much pain as I was, but still she wiggled and stomped and flipped her head in an effort to make her full blonde mane fall back into place and lay just right. OH, OH, a small problem. Her thick blonde fore top now had a large icicle hanging from it. It was hanging right over her left eye, making her crazy. She flipped her head once, then twice; the icicle was relentless and wouldn't let go. Finally... With one last hard flip of her head, the icicle got caught on her blinder and fell to the ground in an explosion of splinters. "There that's better," she grumbled as she straightened herself and gave a large sigh of relief. She wanted to make sure that the entire world knew a beautiful Belgian like herself "had it all together".

The pain and fear was getting the best of her though. She couldn't hide it any longer. Her big snapping dark eyes were a dead give away. They were snapping and crackling just like lighting bolts as she tried to contain her anger. Tipper was real mad... and couldn't contain herself any longer. She blurted out in a half scream, half-crying voice; "I just hate that fire engine and those show off horses. They always get to go first and run the fastest. Here you are, being a famous horse and all... they should have more respect for you; and of course, for me... because I help you pull this carriage." I snapped right back at her, "Wait one minute there, young lady. First of all we are pulling a wagon... not a carriage, and second of all, one of those horses you are referring to in that sassy little voice of yours... is my best friend Jerry. He is definitely not a show off." At the same time I was speaking as harshly as I could to her I was also thinking to myself well... he always was kind of a show off, especially with the fillies. Everything came so easy for Jerry and everyone always admired him. But I was not going to tell Tipper that and give her the satisfaction of being right. I continued to tell her, "What they do is much more important than what we are doing; they save houses and people from burning. All we do is deliver goods. Now... don't go getting your tail feathers in an uproar Tipper... I believe our job is an important one too!"

"Well... I think the fact that we strut and look pretty is just as important." She answered, using as lady-like a voice as she could muster. I laughed at the young filly and said, "I guess so, but you know my friend Jerry and I, well... we go back a long way... to when pretty was something none of us had ever heard of or cared about."

About that time our handler gave us a cluck. We gathered ourselves up, swallowed a deep breath of air to let the pain subside, then took a big step forward with a gentle shake to push our harnesses back into place. With another big step forward we were moving out as if nothing had ever happened. The grayness of the day was surrounding us again. One more time my thoughts slipped back into the past and that haunting feeling of fear I felt during the days Jerry and I were lost and not sure if we would live even one more day. Such vivid thoughts brought on a shiver which ran through my whole body. I thought to myself, boy, winter could be real hard on us horses. My thoughts were getting deep and dark and they made me want to blurt them out in a loud shout, but I didn't want to scare Tipper, so I thought I would just try talking to her about them a little.

"You know," I said to Tipper, "Jerry is the other half of what you call me famous for. You see, there were two of us stranded in the forest that freezing snowy winter, not just me. Jerry and I were to-gether as a team and we stayed a team through it all. We had to, we had to be strong and brave and support each other."

"Really? what do you mean," she asked as the last of the volunteers went racing past and around us. She added to her thought, in her usual sassy tone, "I sure wish we could go see the fire and watch how fast the horses get unhooked from the engine. Nobody ever unhooks us that fast. But any way... what do you mean you had to be strong and brave... tell me... I must know."

I continued my story, " It goes back a few years now. At that time, Jerry and I belonged to another hard working man."

My voice choked up with a huge gulp as we turned the corner where we found ourselves face to face with the smoke and huge flames coming from the house down the street. The red, orange and blue flames where shooting what seemed to be a mile up into the sky. The heat from the fire was so intense that we could feel it a whole block away. We both shuddered at the sight of it. We paused and sat back into our harnesses for a second. Fire is one thing us horses are terri-fied of. The driver clucked us up and encouraged us to keep moving. As we started out again we could feel the warmth from the fire on our faces and chests, it was pleasantly warm and felt real good, giving how cold it was that day. The smoke caught our attention, because it looked real scary. It was very dense and black and had a terrible strong smell to it. There was smoke and ashes falling all around us. The smoke, because of the inversion of the air that morning, was floating to the ground like a big black velvet curtain. It looked like a wall, that no one could get through.

Then suddenly... to our amazement and awe, the black choking curtain of smoke parted, as if it had draw strings on it and the show was about to begin. Out of the middle leaped Jerry and the other fire horses. They were bigger than life, and bolder and more beautiful than you could imagine. They were covered with foaming sweat and their nostrils were spread open like fire-breathing dragons. The sweat blew off of them in plumes of flying foam and their hoof beats sounded like gunfire; bang, bang, and bang as they hit the pavement. Their breath filled the air and it sounded like a windstorm from the north. Their manes and tails were flowing into the air and breaking the smoke away as they came. The sight of them was breathtaking and one of the most exciting things you can watch a horse do. They are the elite of the horse working force. They make us proud to have four legs. Jerry was the biggest, boldest and the proudest of the whole team. As he went bombing by he looked over and spotted me. He shouted above the roaring noise and said, "Hi Tex! Hey it is sure good to see you. Boy after a run like that one, I almost miss the good old days. Hey, hey, hey..... who is the cute little filly beside you there?"

Tipper blushed and said to me in an admiring tone," Well, I guess those fire horses are important after all. They were kind of beautiful coming out of that dark black smoke weren't they? They really must be quite brave to go that close to our dreaded enemy, the fire."

Jerry and the other fire horses never slowed down or missed a step; they just kept trotting on past us. I was thrilled to know Jerry hadn't forgotten me. I knew right away that Jerry had just wowed another girl. He does have the gift!

Our handler clucked to us and reassured us that it was okay to go on. He turned us onto another street, short of all the commotion, so we could finish our delivery. By this time Tipper was totally intrigued about Jerry and wanted to know more about him; and I guess, the story about us.

She said," Boy, I still think those fire horses were kind of beautiful coming out of that dense, black smoke, especially your good friend

Jerry, don't you?"

I grunted back, "You just made that same comment a minute ago."

"I know," she said, "but they were beautiful, don't you think... huh, don't ya... huh... don't ya think?" Her excitement about Jerry and the fire horses led her to start asking me more about Jerry, in a non stop barrage of questions. I wasn't answering her, to her satisfaction, so she started asking me about the whole story; when Jerry and I were a team, and about when we were lost. She kept asking and asking, the whole rest of the trip.

In her best pleading voice she asked one more time, "Please, puh-leeease...Tex, won't you tell me about you and Jerry, and about that winter of 1900. I really want to hear the story about how you survived it all."

I got real quiet and refused to answer her. I also ignored all her many questions. I thought I would let her stew a little, being's she was kind of sassy earlier. I just silently walked along pulling our load beside her. I think I was kind of getting to her..... ha ha.

That night, after we were taken back to the barn and put in our stalls, Tipper shouted to the rest of the horses, "Hey you guys; let's make Tex tell us the tale of him and Jerry and how they became the famous Hungry Horses!" About half of the horses already knew my story. They had lived around Jerry and me awhile and were pretty well versed on the whole thing. But Tipper and her young friends had never heard it. That started me to thinking, it wouldn't hurt these youngsters to learn about a few things like real true friendship, and it sure wouldn't hurt me to tell my tale. In fact, I kind of liked talking about it. Maybe it would help me shake off any of my future bad thoughts about it. I asked my old friends in the barn what they thought and they agreed with me. They said I had a lot of good lessons to teach all these young horses.

"Well," I said as I swallowed my first mouth full of oats, "it is a long story. Starting way back when Jerry and I were just kids on our father's ranch."

"Just get to the brave and strong stuff Tex, I don't care about anything else, and I can't wait any longer!" Tipper said in her disrespectful whine.

I sharply snapped back at her, " Brave and strong Tipper... those were words we didn't need or even understand back then!" My hoof stomped on the barn floor and she surely caught the drift that I was offended by her rudeness. "You need to learn about our background so you can truly understand and appreciate just what becoming brave and strong stands for."

"Ooooh... Ok... all right... I will try to be patient." she said meekly as she was pushing by the other young horses to position herself closest to me. The rest of the young horses gathered up beside her and around me and my old friends found themselves a nice soft mound of straw to lie on.

They all knew my story quite well, and knew it would take a while to tell it, so they wanted to get themselves nice and comfortable before I started my long story of back when I was a freight horse. They were proud old horses and didn't want to admit to the young horses that my tale of terror made even their hair stand up on end every time they heard it.

As I watched them get comfortable, I was thinking that it had been a long hard day and that they had a better idea than I did. Maybe I could just cop out on telling the story.. About that time, a bunch of young, eager and excited colts and fillies were all staring at me with big bright eyes of excitement and anticipation. I couldn't disappoint them, so I started to tell my tale of friendship and hardship to the young crowd

Chapter 2:
From Race Horse
to Work Horse

I started my story with a feeling of excitement and I wondered if the young horses would be able to relate to it in anyway. I began with when we were just colts; we were having a great time running and playing, eating and sleeping. We had just become two-year-olds and had spent a wonderful childhood free from any cares or worries of the world. The only men we saw were the ones throwing us hay to eat. We were totally unaware of any other way of living.

I was just getting a good start on my story, when the air was cut in half by the loud deep voice of one of the old timers in the barn. His voice bounced off of the beams in the ceiling like a jackhammer when he said, "Hey Tex! Be sure to tell them youngsters all about your career as a racehorse!" Then he let out a long, very loud belly laugh; Ha, Ha, Ha...

Tipper jumped in place, her eyes popped out and grew three times larger than their normal size. She blurted out saying, "You? You were a racehorse? What happened? What are you doing here with us? You should be somewhere warm, running races. Tell us! I can't believe it!" Her questions were coming faster than I could even think, let alone answer." How did you end up a workhorse? Boy Tex, you do have a lot to tell us so hurry, get busy, and fill us in... WOW! What a story."

"If you would shut up for a minute or two I might be able to answer some of your many questions."

My face was red with embarrassment, so I said in a rather soft voice, "Yes, I was supposed to be a racehorse. But, I'll make a long story short, you see my mom, Lory, also known as the Prindiville mare, was a racehorse. She won a race when she was four years old. I understand the race was run in Columbia Falls. She raced against a gray mare called Grey Eagle. She won and her owner, William Prindiville, won $400 dollars which was a whole lot of money back then.

Unfortunately, she never talked much about it, especially to me. I think she had always thought it was no big deal. That is all I could ever get her to tell me about her life before I was born. Anyway, Bill sent her to Deer Lodge to be bred by another fancy racehorse stallion. I sometimes wonder if the banker that ran the operation was as careful with my mom's breeding as he should have been, or maybe I was just a throw back, I don't know. All I do know, is that as a two-year-old, I showed a little promise to be able to run. The pasture I grew up in was pretty much all big, heavy, work horses. I guess I thought I was pretty hot stuff because I could outrun all the other colts in that pasture and I guess the man thought maybe I was a runner like my mom. But when I was tried and tested, I was neither fast enough, nor graceful enough."

"I am sorry," Tipper said softly. The room echoed with the same soft moaning sound of sentiment from all the rest of the horses there.

"It is no big deal," I assured all of them, "for my life, as it has gone, has been a pretty darn good one. I love being a workhorse and being here with all of you.

"Anyway, back to my life's journey and my trying to become a racehorse. During this time, as a two-year-old I would have my first, but not my last, meeting with Jerry. We were raised on different parts of the banker's ranch, so our first meeting was when we were taken out of the big pastures and put into the small pasture.. The small pasture was where we would learn life is not just playing and eating.. This was the place we would begin our training to become adult horses.

"Jerry was a big beautiful bay. His color was a very rich dark brown and he had a nice white strip down his face. He had this wonderful presence about himself, his head carriage was just naturally high and proud. He had large round expressive eyes that helped him in his quest to be a prankster and a flirt. He really liked the girls. He was always looking for little ways to cause some havoc and get everyone racing around.

"I, on the other hand, was kind of quiet and stayed to myself a lot. I didn't have any flash to my solid black color and my mane and tail where the same shade as my body, so I didn't have anything that would make me stand out in the crowd. The little snip of white on my face was nothing to brag about.

"The men that worked on this part of the ranch were gentle, kind men and they treated us well. However even their kindness didn't seem to help us very much when it came to the trauma we were all feeling. This new environment brought on a huge culture shock for all of us. The first thing they did to us, after they chased us into a very small pen, was to catch us with a throw rope and put a halter on us.. I will never forget the feeling of helplessness I felt when that rope tightened around my neck. I tried to pull away and run, but the men pushed me into a corner and proceeded to put the halter on me. It was leather and felt like it was squeezing my head into a place it shouldn't have to be. My mouth wouldn't open as wide as usual and it kind of hurt my ears, especially when I pulled back to try to get away from the man. Before they put this halter on me, I could just flip my tail and run away from them. Now they had a hold on me and I couldn't bust loose from them no matter what I did or how hard I tried.

"Come on Tex, let's forget all this growing up and racing stuff and get to the brave stuff!" Tipper wailed, in her usual impatient voice.

"NOW TIPPER... Just one minute here, young lady!" I interrupted her, using my voice of authority, " If you want to hear this story, you are going to have to listen to the whole story, not just the big brave stuff. You need to settle in and listen to what I tell you so you can learn about the two of us, how we ended up together as a team and what took us to the point of having to be brave. There is a lot more to this story than just the exciting stuff. You need to learn about friendship and hard work. Some of these young horses have not had to work yet and this story might help them out some. So... button your lip girl!"

"Now what was I saying? Oh yes, I was real scared, but the man talked to me in a soft voice. My senses were telling me that what was happening wasn't too bad. He stroked me gently on my neck and it did feel kind of good. I wasn't sure if I should let him see me enjoying it or not, so I just stood real still and waited to see what he was going to do next.

"I looked over at my new friend Jerry and saw he wasn't handling things in his usual cool, mischievous manner either. He was standing as still as I was with eyes the size of big red apples. One of the men led me up to where Jerry was being held by another man.

"They started comparing us to each other. They said, "You know, these two boys are about the same size. They look like they might make a good team. If this black boy doesn't make it running we should keep in mind that we could pair him up with this nice big boy. The two of them match up pretty darn good and look like they would make a good team or maybe even a fancy carriage pair."

"We didn't understand at the time what they were saying but we listened and watched them very carefully. Standing beside one another gave us a feeling of security and we thought what was happening wasn't too bad.

"The good feelings were gone real quick and what a shock to our young systems and sense of freedom, when they tied us to this fence. All of a sudden we could not go anywhere no matter how hard we pulled. They left us alone there and we were in for our first hard knock lesson. Both of us had to test those ropes and see if we could get loose and run away. We both pulled back real fast and hard a couple of times. We sat back hard against the ropes and whipped our heads from side to side to try to set ourselves free. It was to no avail and useless to continue. It hurt our heads and tore at our ears, so we both quit pulling back as quickly as we started.

"I looked over at Jerry and he was blurry in my vision I guess I had shaken my head a little too hard. I was taking deep breaths and blowing out air to try to relieve my overwhelming feeling of fear. We could hear the men in the background laughing and saying, Oh, it is so hard to be a horse sometimes. But we still didn't understand that it would be okay. We tried a couple more times just to make sure that we couldn't get away, but that only hurt, so we stood beside each other feeling a little lost, but not really scared anymore. The men came back and patted us. They reassured us that we were doing just fine. They told us that we were good boys.

"Like I said earlier, I was quiet, but I was a very smart kind of fella, what I saw I did not forget. So, I watched very carefully how the man had tied the ropes to the fence. As soon as the men left to have dinner, I put my teeth onto that rope, and I pulled and I tugged, and I tugged and I pulled, until I untied myself... Hurray! I was free from bondage; it felt so good to be free. I shook my head and bounded around in the nice tall, fresh, green grasses. I bucked and kicked and thought I was pretty smart. The smell of the grass got the best of me though, so I dropped my head and proceeded to start eating the sweet fresh tasting grass. I was sure this must be heaven. The grass tasted better to me than it ever had before.

"My moment of bliss became shattered, as I heard loud persistent noises coming from the fence. I heard Jerry shouting in a whisper to me, Hey man, how about getting me untied? I could sure use a nibble of that nice, fresh, green grass along with you.

"I wasn't sure if I should untie him or not. I didn't know him that well and I didn't know what he would do once I did untie him. But, what the heck, I thought, he seemed like a really cool guy and I wanted to be his friend. So I did it... I untied him. Boy, was that ever a mistake! As soon as he was loose, he went right over and opened the gate to the big corral where all the other horses were. He hollered out to all of them, 'Come on guys, green grass and lots of it!' I swear, I never saw a bunch of horses move so fast in my whole young life. I guess that green grass looked pretty good to all of them too. They came busting through the gate all together in one massive group. My goodness... it was a free-for-all; there were legs, tails, manes and heads flying every direction. The dust must have billowed up toward the sky at least three feet into the air. The quiet of the evening was shattered with the on coming rush of noise from the crowd. How they all got out together, through that one small gate and so fast, I will never know. The fillies, of course, all thought Jerry was pretty clever and flirted with him as they flew by to the grass.

"By this time, everyone was making so much noise, that it was inevitable that the men would hear us from the cook shack... and sure enough they did.

"You guessed it, boy, did we ever get into a lot of trouble. It was only a matter of minutes and here came the men from the cook shack. When I look back now, it truly was a sight to see. As they came bursting out of the cook shack they were trying to pull their boots on. They were hopping on one foot, pulling on their boots and trying to keep hold of their lariats all at the same time. Some of them had food flying out of their mouths and others had coffee dribbling down their chins. They were coming fast and hard with lariats being thrown in all directions. All of our oh so grateful friends were high tailing it back into the big corral and leaving us to the mercy of the cowboys. They were yelling at the top of their lungs at all of us. They stumbled and fell and yelled and cursed. After chasing us awhile, the men caught us and tied us back up to that same dumb ole fence. This time they tied us with a knot I could not undo. They finished chasing all the other horses back into the big corral and as the girls went flying past us, they thanked Jerry for such a good time. 'Jerry,' I thought, 'Hey, what about me? I am the one that got loose first and untied him. If it hadn't been for me he would have stayed tied to that dumb ole fence and I would still be enjoying a nice quite satisfying dinner!' But as usual, Jerry, was the hero with the girls.

"Our punishment for causing the fiasco was to be left tied to that darn ole fence all night. So... there we stood, tied beside each other all night long. We had nothing to do and no one else to talk to. We started to share our hopes and dreams with each other and came to an understanding that we were more alike than not. That night became the start of our great friendship. We stood there in the dark with the bright moon and stars above and around us. We laughed over and over again about how funny the men looked chasing after all of us. We also reflected on how nice the girls looked in the moonlight. They were coming over and comforting us during our long hours of repentance.

"The following morning, we were untied. Our training started out to be pretty simple, and kind of fun. The men taught us to walk, trot and canter on a lead rope and to stop on command. We were getting smarter and pretty full of ourselves. We thought that being an adult horse was not a very hard job after all.

"The next morning I received a very harsh, rude awakening. I was taken away from my new friend Jerry and the rest of the young horses we had been in training with. We all protested with loud whinnies to each other, but the men ignored our pleas. I was taken to another part of the ranch. It had fancy stalls and barns and a lot of new people and horses. I was scared and didn't know what was going to happen to me. They shoved me into one of the stalls where they just left me without a word. These men that worked here were not gentle and as easy going as the first men that I had known. In the morning they came and took me to a small round pen. I felt so lost and so confused. They didn't waste a minute, as soon as the gate was closed, they put a little piece of leather something on my back. I heard one of the men call it a saddle. The little leather thing felt funny on my back, so I tried real hard to buck it off of me, it would not budge. Then they grabbed my ear and bent it over in half. One of the men held it real tight, it hurt so bad all I could do was stand as still as a statue. I didn't have a chance to figure out what they were doing to me, let alone be able to figure out what they wanted from me. All of a sudden a man jumped up on my back and kicked me real hard in the side. It scared me so bad all I could think of was I had to try to get him off of me. All I could do was jump and buck real hard. My fear was growing in leaps and bounds as I bucked. I realized that I had no control over what was happening to me and tripped and fell. They hit me and made me get up, I bucked again and I fell again. The men shouted at me and hit me again, and again. I was so confused, they weren't talking to me or trying to let me know what they wanted from me. I became exhausted and out of breath. The sweat was dripping off of me like rainwater. I only had enough strength left in me to drop my head to the ground. There I stood, feeling broken and shattered. My body shook and my heart felt like it was breaking. It was pounding so hard that it hurt in my chest and all the way up into my eyes. Everything they were doing to me was so fast and furious. Before I could even catch a breath, they made me walk out with the man on my back. I accepted it, but I didn't feel comfortable about it. I just didn't understand any of it, especially the man on my back. Then they ripped the saddle off of me and put me back into that dark old stall, were I couldn't see anybody else. I felt so alone and so bewildered. All I could do was hear them talking about me falling down and they had their doubts I would ever run. One of them said, 'I think we are just wasting our time on this one. He sure isn't anything like his mom.' My mom, I thought, what are they talking about I am not like my mom. I just didn't understand what they were expecting of me. I was thinking I sure wished my mom was here right now. It seemed like the longest night of my life."

Tipper had been quiet for what must have seemed like hours to her, but now, she just had to put her two cents in. "Oh! So this is the part where you almost became a race horse," she laughed.

I ignored her nasty little comment and went on with my story. "Before the sun came up the next morning, they came and got me. As they were leading me out of that dark, dingy stall I could catch strange smells and sounds all around me. I watched the mist rising gently up off of the ground and in the distance, I could barely see a funny looking road that was fenced in. My fear started to build.. The closer we got to that funny road the more my senses were taking over. The smells were of fresh dirt and grass. My ears were picking up the sound of hoof beats. It sounded as if a hundred other horses were running straight towards me. The sound kept getting louder and I felt my heart beating with the rhythm of their gaits. It grew faster and louder, I could feel the ground beneath my feet moving and all of a sudden they were flying right past me, and I couldn't help myself; I had to try to turn and run away. The man held me tight and made me stay put as they went running by us. They were going so fast I could barely make out their shapes. All I was sure of was that they were horses and they were running around on that funny little road. My brain was jumping from one thought to another and I still did not know what the heck they wanted from me.

"At that moment a pretty gray horse came up beside me. He brushed up against me and when I felt him, my skin rippled from the tops of my ears down to my hoofs. I was so scared I didn't know who or what to run away from. So I tried to talk to him to ease my fear, but he just ignored me and acted like I was bothering him. That sure didn't help ease my mind or my body; I felt so alone and all I wanted was to go back to my old friends. He was nothing like my friends back at the pasture and he sure was not like my friend Jerry. My fear kept building with every step I took. By this time we were on that funny road with the fence around it. The men came over and threw another man on my back. I bolted and tried to run, but the man on the ground held me tight and in place. At that moment I realized that I had something hard in my mouth. I consoled myself by remembering it was a snaffle bit like they used in my earlier training with Jerry. Oh, how I wished he was there right then, to help me and to talk me through this. He was a friend I could trust and he made me feel brave. Like I said earlier... everything these men did was at a fast and furious pace. My mind was in a fog and I was trying to clear my thoughts and figure out what they wanted from me. I found myself standing beside the other horse on this funny looking road. The man on my back kicked me real hard in my side. The other horse took off at a dead run, so I did the same. I had no idea what we were running from, but I ran as hard as I could anyway. My thoughts flashed back to being loose in the pasture, and for a brief moment I thought, 'this might be fun. It is going to be like racing the other colts to the watering hole.' But the other horse took off so hard and fast that I soon realized that this was not a game. It was nothing like the pasture races for fun. We only ran this hard if something bad was trying to get us. When we had to run this hard we usually knew what we were running from. Here I was being asked to run for no good reason. Try as I might, I couldn't keep up with the other horse. He cut in front of me to get close to that fence that was beside us. I realized we were turning a corner and I tried real hard to keep my footing. I was getting pelted in the face with chunks of dirt; it stung my nose and face. I hated getting hit, so I tried real hard to catch that horse and pass him. No matter how hard I tried I was not able to catch him. But thank goodness after I stumbled a little he got far enough ahead of me that the dirt chunks quit hitting me in the face. I was getting so tired of running that I just wanted to stop and lay down. But the man on my back kept kicking me and hitting me. I tried to keep up the pace, but just couldn't, even though he was hitting me as hard as he could. The pain was a strong driving force of encouragement, but I just couldn't keep up that fast pace. I started to slow down even though the man on my back protested. Finally he stopped me. I stood trying to catch my breath, feeling like I was a hundred years old. As I stood there trying to get a good solid breath of air, I thought to myself, this must be what my mother had to live through. No wonder she would never talk about it to me. I wondered to myself, 'did she hate this as much as I am hating it?' The gray horse came back and stood beside me. He finally spoke to me. 'Wasn't that great? I always feel so free and good after a nice run like that. Boy... you sure don't run like your mom, she would have probably run me into the ground. How she loved to run, especially in the early morning. Are you sure you're a racehorse? You sure don't act like one, and come to think of it, you don't look like one either. You're too heavy and muscular!'

"The man jumped off of me and yelled something to another man who came and got me off of that funny road. I was starting to get my breath back and my mind was starting to clear. My thoughts jumped back to my mother. 'She must have loved doing this,' I thought. I can't understand why, but that gray horse said she did. I wonder why I don't like it and why I am not fast like her? Remember, I said earlier that I don't know how careful they were when they bred my mom. They also had some very good work horse stallions on this place, too. Who knows? Maybe they thought that I was born a race-horse, but maybe, in reality, my daddy was not the stallion they thought. I just know I can't and don't like to run!"

The barn was dead quite and I could hear my breathing, it was coming in short, loud, bursts, from my nostrils. I guess I got tired, just from talking about that running stuff.. Just then, everyone in the barn listening to my story kind of sighed in a tone of sympathy for me. Then in a melodic tone the laughter started soft and grew into a roar, especially from the old timers. Tipper had tears running down her face, she was laughing so hard, and in a giggling tone she said, "I could just see you trying to dodge all those clumps of dirt flying at you, and I bet that man trying to ride you ended up with a head ache. I bet that was the shortest race horse career on record. Ha Ha Ha"

"Ok, Ok, that's enough out of all of you. I may not be a racehorse, but I bet I can out pull any of you in this barn."

The old timer that started this whole thing laughed and said, "Well you got that right." After everyone had a good laugh, I continued with my story.

"As fast and furious as they had come and got me, they took me back. It was all so quick and different. I started out confused and ended up just as confused. That very day they took me back to the other part of the ranch and back to my friends in the pasture. Jerry came running up to me and greeted me with all the enthusiasm he could muster. He looked me up one side and down the other. 'My goodness what happened to you, you look terrible.'

"I blurted out the whole story talking so fast that I think I ran all my words together into one big jumble. Jerry just stood there frozen, looking at me, I don't think he understood what happened anymore than I did. But he had a good laugh at me just like all of you are having.

"The very next day the men came and got us and I was put back into training with Jerry like I had never left. 'These humans are a funny lot!' I thought. But I was so relieved that I was back I didn't care that our training continued."

Chapter 3:
Training Can Be Pretty Darn Scary...

"My trust in the human race had been shattered a bit, so I was a little standoffish and a little jittery about continuing training. Despite my silly fears our training started going well and I was building small amounts of confidence, until the day I was first introduced to and hooked to a wagon.

"I was taken out of the corral alone, so not having Jerry to lean on for security was my first worry. As they rolled the wagon into position it squeaked and groaned and made noises I had never heard before. It sounded and looked real scary. It looked so much bigger and heavier close up than it did when we saw it from a distance. I thought to myself, 'oh... I can't do this... I just can't.' The feeling of fear had penetrated every muscle and bone in my body; it was almost too much to bear. I wanted my friend Jerry to be beside me so bad. Of course the men couldn't know what I was feeling or what was going through my mind. So I tried to imagine that Jerry was standing there right beside me. It gave me comfort for a fleeting moment. But then the men came walking up to me bringing all these leather straps and buckles and stuff. They were making even stranger noises than the wagon had. The harness seemed to be bigger and a lot more than they had ever put on me before. The leather felt strange and its smell was new to me. It made a squeaking noise while they were positioning it on my back. It didn't hurt or anything, it just felt kind of heavy on my back and face. But that thing they stuck up under my tail, well! let me tell you, that was not only a horrible feeling, but it was the most embarrassing thing I had ever had done to me. I knew I had to just grin and bear it, and eventually it felt okay."

About this time, Tipper blurted out, saying, "Oh Tex, that was the worst thing about my training too! I just never had the courage to tell anyone, because of it being so embarrassing. Oops... I am sorry Tex, go on with your story."

I looked at Tipper in awe... she was actually a little polite.

"They called the darn thing a crupper and I thought it was the crappiest thing a man could do to a horse. It was real humiliating at first, stuck up under my tail like that and all."

"Hmmmm ahahh..." "Yes indeedie." "That's for sure," I heard softly coming from the old horses relaxing in their straw.

I let the sound effects drift by me and went on to say. "At the time I didn't know how important a crupper is, especially when you are trying to hold a load back like we had to do this morning. All I knew was that it was a foreign object making me very uncomfortable"

I was also thinking, almost out loud by now, 'Oh my! What us horses have to do to make the men in our lives happy.'

I went on to say, "I was real nervous about what was being done to me and what was to be expected of me. It sure didn't help to have all the other horses standing over on the other side of the fence watching the whole procedure. I was young and anxious to please, but I was also very scared. It took a little time but I was starting to accept and really understand the reasons for all the stuff they had just put on me. I honestly think the bridle was the worst though. The cold metal bit that they stuck in my mouth was solid and hard. It didn't bend like the snaffle bit they had used before. It felt so much heavier. The blinders made it so I couldn't see things the way I was used to. My eyes were straining and they felt like they wanted to try to jump out of my head in order to see like I normally did. The blinders kept me from seeing a lot of things, especially what they were doing behind me. No matter how big I opened my eyes I still could not see anything. By this time my whole body was starting to shake. My legs felt like rubber and I just wanted to let out a squeal and run.

"It didn't help the situation that it had started raining and the ground was starting to get very muddy and slippery. My fear was building and about to get the best of me. They slowly lead me up to that big old heavy wooden contraption that they called a wagon. I had only seen wagons from a distance before. Now here I was standing right next to one. It looked pretty scary so I let out a little snort. The man patted me and said it was okay, don't be afraid. Then he turned me around and started to back me up into the shafts on the wagon. I was so scared, but the man kept talking to me in a kind voice. I worked real hard to settle my fears of this big wooden thing. I had dragged poles before, but they were light and didn't make all the noise that this wagon made.

"You know us horses and the way our natures are; we want to be accepted and appreciated by human beings. So I kept listening to the man and trying real hard to stand still and be brave. I looked over at the fence and Jerry was trying to reassure me from afar. I was settling in and starting to feel a little braver when, all of a sudden, a huge bolt of lighting flashed what seemed to be the brightest light I had ever seen. It struck the ground with a loud crack and in an instant we felt and heard a very loud rolling boom of thunder. It made my hair stand up on end and I felt the electricity flowing through my body. I didn't know what to do, I was so scared, so I did what all self-respecting good horses do. I jumped straight into the air just as high and as far forward as I could and I started to run for my life. I ran and ran hard. I think if the race horse men could have seen me at that very moment, they would have wanted to keep me as a racehorse. I ran straight away from that scary contraption that they were trying to hook me to.

The man shouted, 'Whoa!'

"Whoa! 'What does that mean,' I thought, I don't remember or understand that word for some reason. All I knew was that I was scared to death, and the man's shouts sounded like he was real mad at me and that scared me even more so there was only one thing to do and that was to run harder and faster than I already had been running. So I did just that, I ran away from all those things that were scaring me. I ran as fast as my young legs could carry me. As I was running I could hear Jerry over the fence laughing like some kind of a mule or something. 'How could he laugh at me at a time like this,' I thought. Boy, when you need your friends they just desert you and make jokes and laugh at you. Then I heard him saying, while he was laughing 'Hey Tex, look behind you. You're dragging a cowboy along with you. He looks like a flopping fish on the end of a fishing pole.'

"That scared me even more, so I shifted into a higher gear and ran even faster. All of a sudden, what seemed to be the biggest man I had ever seen in my young life, jumped in front of me and yelled, 'Whoa!' real loud and with a lot of authority in his voice. Well right then and there I remembered what that word, 'whoa,' meant. I stopped as short as I could. The man I was dragging along behind me slid right up and into the back of my legs. But believe me I didn't move a muscle, I just stood there and shook like a tree blowing in a windstorm.

"Like I said, the man was kind. So he didn't get too mad at me. By this time Jerry had everyone in the pasture looking and laughing at the man that I had dragged through the mud. As I stood there shaking and looking at him I had to admit, Jerry was right, the man looked real funny with mud all over him. The mud was so thick on his face that you couldn't even tell if he had a nose or mouth or eyes. His shirt was torn and he had lost one boot along the way. The mud was dripping off of him in large gooey clumps. I probably should have been afraid of him, but he was not nearly as scary as what I had just gone through.

"The other men that were helping him were laughing real loud. They picked him up and flung him into the watering trough. I was still shaking and snorting a little, but watching that man get a bath sort of soothed my nerves and I had to laugh inside myself, cause he sure did look funny. Well needless to say, that was the end of training for that day."

As I was finishing my statement I noticed that one of the youngest of the horses listening had eyes as big as saucers. "Is training really that scary?" he said with a quiver to his voice.

"No, not all the time, but I think every horse has to face a demon or two. But don't you worry, you will do just fine and if you listen to your elders, you can save yourself a lot of unnecessary problems. Now don't go letting your mind warp your thinking about training. It won't hurt you a bit."

After settling his worries I continued on. "By the time I got back to the pasture Jerry had told everyone what I had done. It kind of made me a big shot in the eyes of the fillies. For a moment or two I was the center of attention and all the fillies where gathered around me and telling me I had put on a good show for them. I thought to myself, 'soooo... this is why Jerry is always showing off for the girls. This feels pretty darn good!' I puffed up and strutted around for a little while thinking I was somebody. While I was in the middle of my glory and had all the girls around me I had my first glimpse of a mare that would own my heart to this very day. She was the most beautiful filly I had ever seen. In the crowd of other mares she stood out like a beam of sunshine. She was a classic golden Belgian. Her mane and tail were as white as snow and they floated like silk as she passed by me. She turned and the wind gently blew the hair from her face to reveal the biggest, kindest, darkest eyes I had ever seen. I was lost in them and didn't want to be found. Her voice sounded like the melody from a meadowlark. She shyly spoke, 'Hi, I am Madeline Rose. You were wonderful today, Tex.' Then she disappeared behind some other horses."

The barn was quiet except for a warm melodic sigh.

I continued on with my story, surprisingly without any interruption from little Miss Tipper.. I felt that the young horses were learning a little something from me.

"Well," I said, "The very next day the sun was out, and they came and got me to try again. The night before I had made up my mind, and with strong support from my friend Jerry, this time when they hooked me up to that contraption, I would act real big and brave and pull like I had done it all my life. I just knew in my mind that Madeline and all the girls would be watching me, and I just knew they would be so proud of me if I did it right. So I did just that; I backed right up to that thing and let them hook me up. Even though my knees were knocking, I pulled that wagon along behind me like I knew what I was doing. I looked over expecting to see all the girls watching me, but to my surprise they were all out in the pasture following Jerry around. Oh who am I kidding; it didn't surprise me at all. Those girls just loved Jerry. I purposely looked for Madeline. I didn't see her there with Jerry, so I kind of felt better about that. I dreamed she only wanted me.

Jerry of course had watched my entire trauma so when it was his turn, he strutted right up to that wagon and went to pulling straight away just like a king. I must say, he did look pretty sharp, all done up in that shiny leather harness. He carried himself in a manner that would make any of us jealous. He looked proud, strong and beautiful. You could tell by the way the men were talking, he had impressed them completely. I dreamed of being just like him someday.

"While I was watching Jerry and all he did, to try to learn something, I felt a soft touch on my shoulder. I turned to look straight into Madeline's eyes. I was instantly lost in them. She had to say hi twice, before my brain kicked in and I realized I wasn't dreaming. She spoke in such a soft gentle voice but I heard it as if it was a blow horn. She said, 'Tex, I think you do just as good a job as Jerry does, and besides, you don't use your job to show off with.. I like Jerry, but he is too big and bold for me.' I know I almost fell to my knees as she kept talking.

"I hope you don't mind me being rather forward, but I was wondering if you would like to join me in the creek. It is so nice and cool, and feels so good on a hot day like today."

"I stuttered back, 'SSSSUUUURRREEEE' I instantly forgot about Jerry and what ever he was doing. We spent that first day enjoying each other standing in the nice cool creek."

Tipper swooned and said, "I think you fell in love, Tex"

"Maybe, Tipper. Maybe." I answered in a quiet, soft voice.

"I always worked hard to pattern myself after Jerry. It all came so easy and natural for him. When we were out in the pasture together, he was never too proud or busy to teach me the proper way to carry myself and help me learn the different gaits.. He was beautiful and he knew it. But he always treated me with respect and kindness.. We were becoming true friends. The summer past, Jerry and I became real good at our work. We were quite a team. We pulled together in unison, and that made the work real even, so one of us didn't have to carry the whole load on his own. Our gaits matched so we could cover a lot of ground together and we were one of the strongest teams on the place.

"But I must tell you it wasn't always easy. At first, our gaits didn't match at all. Jerry floated across the meadow and I kind of bull-dozed my way across it. I felt like I had eight legs instead of four. Jerry was determined though to get us traveling together. His patience and expertise with giving a perfect example helped me to get rid of my extra pair of legs.

"Now let me tell you about this one-day. We were out in the middle of the pasture practicing and Jerry was putting the ole pressure on me to keep up. I was just starting to feel my legs getting stronger and doing what I wanted them to do. I was even feeling like I looked almost as good as Jerry. One thing though, I couldn't look up from the ground cause when I did I would always trip and fall flat on my face.

"Remember Madeline, the beautiful filly, we were becoming the best of friends. She was always nice to me and would stand by me in the cool creek. While our feet were being cooled and refreshed, we would stand side by side, but head to tail. I would put my head and neck up over her back and reach across and scratch her with my teeth ever so gently. She would do the same for me. Jerry flew by one day and said in a laughing tone 'You two look like a pretzel when you do that!' Sometimes it would feel so good to Madeline, that she would stop scratching me. She would stretch her neck out as far as she could, then she would point her nose towards the clouds in the sky, and roll her lip up. It looked funny, but I knew I was making her feel good, by the sounds of her gentle sighs. We also would use our tails to keep the flies off of each other's faces. And what a beautiful face she had. We always ate together at the hay mound. She loved standing under the one and only big tree we had in the pasture. That was her tree and none of the other horses ever challenged her for it. She was a lovely mare, but she also had a very fast, dead aim kick. Especially when it came to her tree. I was always her welcomed guest though.

We spent many days relaxing and standing under that silly thing."

"Tex, had a girl friend! Yes he did, oh yes he diiiddd." Tipper sang out, "I don't believe it, I just don't believe it! It sounds like she was a beautiful Belgian, just like me!" she mused. "Was she, was she... oh was she as pretty as me?"

"That is enough out of you missy," I retorted.

"Now! Back to me and Jerry and our practice session. Like I said, I was feeling pretty good about myself. When I heard my good ole buddy Jerry saying, 'Hi Madeline, how are you this bright sunny morning?' Well, I was concentrating so hard on what I was doing and so afraid to look up that, yes, you guessed it, I plowed right into the middle of her like the giant bulldozer I was. I knocked her right to her knees. Then I slid about ten feet on my rear end, right up to her favorite and only tree in the pasture. There I laid, flat on my back with my big ole clumsy legs wrapped around that tree. I was looking straight up towards the branches. My first thought was, 'well this is a fine mess I have gotten myself into.' It was not a very pretty sight to see, I am afraid. Madeline got up right away and ran over to me to see if I was okay. As I struggled to untangle my legs and crawl back up to my feet, she was her usual sweet self.

"She said, 'Oh my, I am so sorry, I didn't mean to get into your way like that. I know how hard the two of you are working to become a good team. Oh, please forgive me.'

"Beings that I was a gentleman of good character and all, I thought I would just go ahead and let her take the blame for our accident, so I said back to her, " Oh that's okay, I know you didn't mean to be in our way." What a man... huh! I should have been shot on the spot for not being honest and putting the blame where it really should have been, on my big ole clumsy feet and me. Jerry, on the other hand, was not only good at his job of pulling; he was also a real gentleman to the ladies. He cornered me and scolded me for my actions. Then he made me go back over and apologize to Madeline and explain it was me, not her, that caused the accident.

"You know, I learned a lot more that day than just putting my feet in the right place. You see, friends help friends to become better than what they are. Friends show you and tell you if you are messing up real bad, and Jerry was my true friend. Madeline in all her grace and beauty accepted my apology like the lady she was.

"Jerry and I continued to work hard together. Through hard work and a good friendship we became one of the most sought after teams in the region."

I stopped telling my story for a minute and glanced around. The young horses in the barn where all standing patiently, listening with curious young ears and waiting for me to continue. I glanced at all their eyes and felt warm inside and knew that I was doing the right thing in telling them my story.

Just then I realized, beings I was doing all the talking, my oats were not getting eaten, so I took a deep breath and then grabbed another bite of the sweet smelling oats and savored their flavor. Oh, how I loved my oats!

Chapter 4:
A New Life

"The day came when the man felt our time with him was over. His job was completed, he had raised us, trained us and now would sell us to another man. Our training was completed and he felt we were the best working team he had ever trained. He knew we were the best and strongest team in the whole county. That made us valuable. He knew he would make big money from us. We were to be advertised and sold as a team to another man, or so we thought. Come to find out, I was already owned by another man, the man that owned my mother. His name was William Prindiville and he was from a place called the Flathead Valley and a town site known as LaSalle.

I think when Bill first got there to take me home he was kind of disappointed that I didn't turn out to be a good racehorse like my mom. But the training men started telling him what a good work horse I had become, and that I had a lot of heart. They told him I would do what ever they asked of me. The men also told him about Jerry and what a good team we made together. They said we were unbeatable as a team and together there was not another team on the place that could beat us in any task laid before us. Bill started to think, me being a good work horse might be a better thing after all.

The men told Bill he should think about buying Jerry and keeping us together.

"I think that banker fella kind of knew he had maybe messed up, and I think he felt bad also. He told Bill he knew he could make a lot of money off of us as a team. He gave Bill a real good deal on Jerry. I think he knew that Bill was a smart man and could have probably got him into a lot of trouble over my breeding pooh pa. But anyway, a deal was made and the inevitable was going to take place. We would get to stay together as a team, but we were going to have to leave our happy home.

"When the day came that we found out we would be leaving the next morning with Bill, I thought my heart would break. This meant that I would have to say good-bye to Madeline. So that night we stood as close as we could to each other. We talked and nuzzled and re-membered all the fun we had out in the big pasture. We talked about the cold creek and how much better the hay tasted because we had each other to eat it with. We both knew that it was going to really hurt, so we tried not to talk about the future or even think about it.

"The next morning Bill came to get us. I made him drag me away from Madeline. We both whinnied and screamed as loud as we could. I pulled back hard a couple of times. But Bill kept me going. I kept whinnying until I couldn't see or hear her anymore. Jerry tried to comfort me. But his words fell on deaf ears. Ears that drooped out of sadness and eyes that would not stop leaking water. My heart was broken for sure. I wish we could talk in human language so we could tell the man that we had feelings and that our hearts could break just like theirs. It was the worst day of my life, and I still wish that I could be with Madeline.

"Jerry, on the other hand, was so excited he could hardly contain himself. He was singing a song with delight in his voice, a new adven-ture. Oh, boy... great new adventures.

'Tex, just think we are setting out for a whole new life. Tons of new girls to meet, and a whole New World to impress with our talents as a team.' His enthusiasm did lift my spirits a little. After a time on the trail and covering several miles we started seeing things that were new and yes, wonderful. I was starting to get excited about our new life, but my heart still was lonesome for Madeline.

"Our new man, William Prindiville's place in the Flathead Valley was quite a ways from where we lived. It took us awhile to get to the new place. When we finally came to the Flathead Valley, we were surprised and pleased. We both thought... wow, this is a place a horse could just die for! So much green grass and fresh water. Looking at what a beautiful place it was, my thoughts went back to my sweet Madeline, and I felt so sad that she wasn't with us. I knew she would love it here, because she always liked standing under that one lonely tree in our old pasture. The tree, was really a perfect place in her thinking and something she expressed to me very frequently.

"What Jerry and I didn't know or understand was, that even though it was a seemingly perfect place, it was mountain country. Mountain country means severe and sudden changes of weather and a lot more snow in the winter. Where we came from it was flat wide open country, it got cold, but the snow all blew away so you could always walk and find something to eat. Little did we know at that time, we were headed for some real tough and scary mountain country lessons."

The silence in the barn was broken with a start, when my little friend, Tipper squealed... "Oh Tex, I have goose bumps. Hurry, hurry tell us the scary stuff!"

"Hold your horses", I told her, (forgive the pun). She was wiggling like a worm on a fishhook as she stood there in the crowd of young horses.

"Settle down," I said. "I will get to the rest of the story in a minute. I need a long cool drink of water. A guy's throat gets kind of dry telling all this stuff."

By this time she had all the rest of the young horses wiggling and squirming just like she was.

"Now... back to what I was saying. What was I saying anyway?"

Tipper chimed in again, "Tex, don't tease, tell us more please, please." The other young horses echoed her sentiment. "Yes please tell us Tex," they all said.

"OK..." I said. "You need to settle down though, cause I have some other stuff to tell you first before we get to the scary stuff."

They all groaned but stopped wiggling and squiggling.

"You know I would have never believed that a place could be so darn pretty. When we came to the top of that pass and started down on the other side I looked out and saw miles and miles of trees and grass and water. It was all sorts of beautiful shades of green. My eyes watered from the beauty of it all. It smelled fresh and sweet like nothing I had ever smelled before. It wasn't dry and dusty like where we had come from.

"In my state of awe, I found myself as usual not watching where I was walking. Jerry had to bump me and say, "Hey, if you fall I fall and I really don't want to have this load run over us. Please, do your job my good friend." Jerry was the rock of our team. He never stumbled and he always knew where we were going to place our feet next. " Hey, I am so sorry," I apologetically said to Jerry. But Jerry had to admit that he had never seen anything so pretty in his life either. We just had to admit we had been flatlanders too darn long. The new sights, sounds and smells helped ease my broken heart. I was now ready for a new life.

"The work in this terrain was a lot harder though. It wasn't flat and open. It had hills and rough road to cross. But we always had something new and exciting to look at. The deer and the elk never scared us much, but those darn old bears could sure give us a start. Jerry was braver than I was when it came to those darn ole bears. So he would hold strong in his harness and that would keep me from bolting and running, which is what my old heart and legs were telling me to do. At times like that, I was sure a wishing I had my moms ability to run, and run fast.

"As that summer wore on we got real good at pulling hills and holding back the loads. Our man, Bill, liked to show us off to all the other freight haulers and of course we did our best to prove him right about us. Bill was an exciting man, he had us working and doing a lot of exciting neat things."

Chapter 5:
The Competition Was Hot

"I remember one day a couple years later; I think that it was around the Fourth of July. Bill was bragging about us as usual, and some folks started gathering to listen to him. One ole boy said, "Bill I think you're pulling my leg and your stories about these two horses are getting pretty darn big."

"So... Bill, in his big, prideful manner of doing things, made a bet with this guy that we could out pull his team or any other team for that matter. He boasted that he knew we could pull the heaviest load, the longest distance. So all the men got busy and set up a competition for us. I don't know if Bill got worried or not, or if he got to thinking that maybe his bragging ended up with us biting off more than we could chew. But to the amazement of everyone, teams started coming in from all over the valley. We ended up pulling against five other teams.

"As they were bringing the teams up I noticed this one particularly beautiful blonde mare. I whispered to Jerry, "Do you think that could possibly be Madeline over there?"

Jerry, not being a bit bashful or anything, yelled, 'Hey Madeline, is that you?' I could have died of embarrassment.

"She said, back to us, 'It sure is me, Gee, it is so good to see you both again. I would like you to meet my team mate and working partner Carol. I think we work together as a team as good as the two of you do. We have accomplished alot together. Carol was quiet and shy, she said 'How do you do.' Of course Jerry put on the old charm and before too long had Carol blushing. While this was going on Madeline kept her attention on me. Tex, how are you? I sure have missed you, and our walks in the creek.'

"I know my face must have turned a brilliant red; Carol's blush was pale in comparison. But I didn't care; it was Madeline, it was really her. I would have never dreamed in a million years that I would get to see her again. Jerry poked me with his blinder on his harness bridle to give me a hard time. I stumbled at that moment being the graceful swan I was. But I didn't care, because my heart warmed with delight to see her again.

"Right then, I knew without a doubt that we had to pull till our hearts blew up, or darn close to it. I wanted to show off for her and show her how mature and strong I had become. It never crossed my mind that I would have to compete against her.

"While we were waiting to get set up for the competition to begin, my friend Jerry was up to his usual antics. He reached over and grabbed Bills gloves from his back pocket as he walked by us. Bill went to the front of us and started to adjust our harnesses. He reached in his pocket for his gloves. When they weren't there he said immediately, 'OK... Jerry, where are my gloves?' Jerry had his head turned and Bill didn't see him holding them. Bill went to turn Jerry's head towards him, which he did but Jerry raised it, so high in the air Bill couldn't reach his gloves. I giggled at how Bill was trying to be ten feet tall and just couldn't hit the mark. He got mad and said, 'Ok... you can keep them then.' Well, the fun was over so Jerry head-butted Bill in the back and gave him his gloves. We all laughed together, we laughed like horses do and Bill roared with his human voice. It was turning out to be a perfect day.

"The pulls started, and we pulled all the loads with ease. We knocked the teams out one after another until there was just one team left. Yup... you guessed it, Madeline and her partner Carol were the only team left for us to beat. By this time most of the early morning had past and the heat of the day was hitting us. I was starting to really sweat and I was tired from the heat and the hard pulls. Jerry was getting tired like I was. We laughed and said wouldn't it be funny if those two girls beat us at our own game here. To make the pull more exciting the men hooked us up to our individual sleds and then placed us side by side to pull simultaneously. The sleds were the heaviest of the day. They were not content with that fact, so now they were adding people to the sled to add the extra weight they wanted. I swear, when I was watching those old beer bellied, bearded fellows climbing on I thought to myself, 'come on guys, give us a break.' The crowd was growing with every team we beat. It had grown very large and loud by now and the men were all betting on their favorite team. Jerry and I were taking very deep breaths trying to get ourselves ready for another pull. Jerry kept leaning over to the girls and telling them funny things like their harnesses didn't match and their hair was a mess. The girls were getting quite put out with him, but he would just laugh and nudge me in a joking manner. While we were waiting for the signal to pull again, we teased and joked and were kidding around on the surface, but our competitive spirits were churning in our minds and our muscles. We planted our feet deep into the soil and looked out the sides of our eyes at those two girls. Who, by the way, were just standing there all calm and collected and they weren't even sweating yet."

Tipper chimed in, "I bet they beat you, huh. Us girls are always stronger than you boys are."

"Well, as a matter of fact Tipper," I said in an irritated voice, "you just wait and see. I will tell you the rest of the story in a minute."

"Ok then what happened, they beat you didn't they? I knew it, I just knew it," she sassed back. "All I can say is that, if they didn't beat you, their harnesses must have broke or something terrible like that."

"Like I said Tipper; Jerry and I hunkered down and dug deep. When they said go, the girls leaped out first and were a smidge ahead of us. We leaned hard into our harnesses and put a strong steady pull into it. That form of pulling had beat all the other teams for us, and now it was keeping us moving steadily forward. We took one solid step after another. The dirt was flying out behind us from the force of each step. Both teams were putting all we had into it. The harnesses were squealing and squeaking from the strain on them. The crowd was yelling for all of us at the top of their lungs. We could tell the girls were starting to get tired. They were straining with all their might into their harnesses and the sweat was popping up all over their bodies. Their handler was slapping the reins on their backs. It sounded like rifle shots. But, try as they might, they were running out of strength. We felt bad but we were guys and we were proud. Our competitive spirits broke loose. We dropped our heads even lower to the ground. Then with an exploding mighty grunt, a huge burst of muscle power, and a will to win, we gave one last big effort. We pulled right up to, and past those girls. They were at the end of their pulling power; they had run totally out of steam. They were down practically on their knees now, pulling with all the strength they had left in them. The sweat was pouring off of them, and us, and the harnesses seemed like they had stretched a mile. When we couldn't take one more step, and all was said and done, we had managed to pull five more feet than they did.

"As soon as I could catch a short breath, I looked over at Madeline, she was totally spent but managed to give me a small wink.

Our muscles were burning and trembling more than they had ever done before. We were hurting from our ears down to our ankles and feet, even our tails hurt, from the strain that we had just put ourselves through. We stood gasping for air, and knew it was the hardest we had ever worked. But it was sure worth it when we watched Bill in all his glory. He jumped and shouted and danced all over the place. He threw his brand new hat straight up into the air. He ran past all the men grabbing his hand to shake it, and came up to the front of us, he patted us and kissed us and told us that we were his SUPER HORSES... I think at that moment in time Bill was glad I wasn't a racehorse. We had a lot to be proud of and the crowd let us know how much they appreciated our hard work. Bill was so proud that I think he was bustin' buttons off of his shirt. We must have won him some money that day, because right off, he brought us a bucket of nice, cool, frothy beer. Bill also took the time to give us a good hard scratch on our chests, while he was taking our harnesses off. That would always put me instantly into la-la land, I would wiggle my lips back and forth in time with his scratching motion. Sometimes I would even return the favor, and reach over his shoulder and scratch his back for him, at the same time he was scratching me. As soon as we were totally cool and dry, he gave us an extra big helping of oats. A perfect reward for a day well done. It was great fun and ended up being a beautiful day in more ways than one.

"After the pull I thought my luck had reached its peak when Madeline's owner tied her to the post right beside mine. I was instantly transported to heaven. She leaned over and touched me with her soft nose and said, "Tex you are the strongest horse I know and if I ever needed to be rescued, I know you would be the one to get the job done." I didn't realize at that moment in time what those words would come to mean to me. They would end up giving me strength and warmth during a time I would have little else. Madeline and I spent the night rubbing noses and scratching each other on the withers. We reminisced about that silly old tree and how protective she was over it. She always made me feel so good. It was a short, but wonderful night of pure bliss; I will cherish it forever.

"Unfortunately for us horses, we don't have any control on how our lives will go. Early the next morning Madeline's owner came and got her. To this very day I have never got to see her again, after that night. My heart still longs to see her beautiful blonde mane flowing down over her neck and swinging in the breeze so softly that it didn't look real."

Tipper of course had to ruin my minute of bliss, with her shrill little voice, she added. "I still think it sounds like she was almost as beautiful as I am."

"Oh Tipper, you and your being beautiful. Is that all you ever think about?" I mused. "Well no! I still want to hear about the scary stuff," she shouted.

"Ok, Ok... I will get to the scary stuff. I hope you are ready to handle what you will hear. But first I need to stretch and shake and get another bite of hay."

The young horses were getting closer to me and crowding in. They all chimed in together and echoed Tippers sentiments, "Yeah... Let's get to the scary stuff Tex, please, we can hardly wait."

Chapter 6:
Oh! That Dreaded Train

"Hey!" I bellowed as loud and as sharp as my voice could go. About three of the colts fell backward and shook their heads in a motion that showed me I got their attention. Even the old horses that were half a sleep jumped to attention. The barn rafters shook and the old owl took flight from his perch.

"How was that for scary stuff?" I said with a haunting laugh. Ha, Ha, Ha...

Tipper reached over and bit my shoulder and said, "Tex cut it out! You scared us half to death."

"Well you said you wanted to hear the scary stuff." I repeated in another haunting laugh. "All kidding aside I better get back to my story. This part might scare some of you; cause I know one horse that was so scared he forgot his own name."

"Oh tell us, who was that?" Tipper asked.

The blue roan horse, Chester, broke out into a roaring laugh and said, "Oh I know who it was." Chester was sometimes my pulling partner and he used to be on the fire department with Jerry. "Say Tex, you want me to tell this part of your story for you?" he offered, "then you can eat the rest of your dinner."

"No, that's ok." I answered. "I started this adventure, so best I finish it."

"During our big pulling contest this man came to Bill and talked to him about hiring us to do some work for him. Bill was real impressed with this guy and agreed to his terms of employment. The man assured Bill that the job would be done by Christmas. We got the feeling the job was going to be a big one by the way the man was flinging his arms around, telling Bill about it. But we weren't for sure what we would be doing.

"Only a couple of weeks passed and we kind of got the feeling our new job was about to start by the way Bill was fixing everything around the place. It seemed he had a feeling of urgency to get things in order around there.

"The next morning when dawn was breaking and we were waking up, I nudged Jerry and said, 'I always love that first ray of light that turns everything kind of blue, and when the sun breaks through the cut in the mountains, it always seems to say, welcome to another glorious day and another great adventure. Don't you agree?'

Jerry was still trying to make me feel better about Madeline having to leave again. So he politely replied, 'yes I do... and I sure am sorry about Madeline having to leave.'

'Let's just concentrate on this new day, ok,' I said.

'Ok,' He muttered, 'let the games begin.'

"We saw the lights come on in the house. It was Jerry's job to whinny first because he had the loudest most obnoxious whinny of us all. Then the rest of us would chime in. Old Bill would come out every single morning to us yelling our heads off. We just knew that our sad cries would make him feel guilty so he would hurry to feed us. Then as Bill would get closer to us with the food, Jerry and I would put our ears back flat, as flat as we could on our heads and we would charge out after all the other horses. Judy and Robyn would run the farthest and the fastest. But Pete and Chester would always make one of us give them a little nip or kick, before they would give in and run away. Oh what fun and what a wonderful way to start each and every day. We thought we were so big and bad. We always got food first. Now, we weren't all bad, we would eventually let everyone else eat too. It was just big fun causing a fiasco at every feeding. Bill had patience with us and just ignored our little game."

Chester had to add, "I won the fight once in awhile and got to eat first."

"Yes Chester you sure did," I agreed. As I looked over Chester's direction I caught a glimpse of my little friend Tipper; she was stealing a bite of my oats. A girl of my own heart I thought.

I went on with my story, "after breakfast Bill took and harnessed us. Of course while he was putting the harness on one of us, the other was poking and pulling and goofing around. Why he let us do that, we didn't know, but he sure made going to work fun. After a few minutes of play and fun he told us we had to get down to business, so he hooked us to the wagon and gave us a cluck to go to work. We were very relaxed and just plodding along, doing whatever Bill requested of us. Neither one of us was paying too much attention to where we were going. Bill didn't seem to be acting any different, so we thought it was going to be another day just like every other day.

"As we moved along I came to the realization that we were starting to getting closer to the town site of Columbia Falls, and I started to get nervous. You see back then, the city scared me a tad, not bad, but enough to make me sweat a little and to give Jerry something to tease me about. As we hit the main part of town, I was starting to do my spooky thing. My good helpful friend Jerry had to say, 'Look out, look over there.'

"He had me jumping away from and seeing things that weren't

really there. Then he would laugh and his whole harness would shake. I always wondered if Bill knew what was going on with us. He never seemed to notice.

We continued right up the main part of town until we reached the railroad tracks. There, Bill pulled us up and parked us real close to those tracks. We had never seen or been that close to them before. We were just standing there relaxing and minding our own business, along with some other teams. Some we knew, like the ones Bill's brother had, Chester and Judy, and some were strange to us. We didn't know them or the men that were with them; they had all sorts of stuff like tents and little wood stoves. So we thought, 'neat... it looks like we are all going camping.' We were talking among ourselves and enjoying the peaceful quiet of the morning when, all of a sudden the ground started to shake. We felt this weird vibration in our feet and legs, and then we heard this loud, screaming, whistle. We saw this huge black, fire-breathing dragon, coming right straight towards us. The clanking noise and immense size of the thing caused us both to jump. Then we heard loud bursts of hissing steam that sounded like it had a giant snake in it. Jerry was totally convinced that this huge black contraption, which was heading straight for us, would devour us. Its huge black wheels looked just like they could chop us up in a million pieces. It was belching and blowing clouds of smoke, soot and steam. As the locomotive rumbled past, the screeching of the air brakes on the cars cut into the cool morning air and caused our hair to stand on end. You know what? My so very brave, nothing-bothers-me friend, Jerry, was trying to jump plumb out of his harness! Bill jumped down off of the wagon and grabbed us. We were both rearing and trying to run backwards with the wagon. We were tossing Bill into the air like he was a limp noodle. Some other guys ran over and helped Bill hold on to us. This was the scariest thing to ever happen to us, so far, in our lives. We were absolutely positive that

that contraption was going to swallow us whole."

The barn was absolutely quiet. I looked over at what seemed to be a hundred huge eyes staring back at me, so I told the colts, "Hold on, it gets even worse!" They all crowded in closer to each other in anticipation of it getting even scarier.

"They finally got us to stop leaping long enough to get us unhooked from the wagon. I started to settle down and get used to all of these new sounds and smells, but my poor friend Jerry just couldn't seem to get himself under control. After Bill got us unhooked from the wagon, he tried to lead us over to that gigantic monster. By this time, Jerry was totally out of control, he was leaping and squatting and doing everything he could to keep from going closer to that thing. He ran circles around and around Bill. I am sure these maneuvers must have made them both terribly dizzy. Some other fellas came over to try to help. Jerry dragged two of the men at least twenty feet up the street, backing away from that thing. I was scared, but also in shock. Watching my normally, very cool friend going through his tremendous panic attack. I forgot all of my own fears, because I never ever thought that Jerry would react in such a way to anything. He was the rock, and always under control, nothing seemed to ever scare or upset him.

"They led me up the ramp and onto the train car. It was open roofed, with sides on it. They led me around on it for a minute or two. I guess I showed them that I wasn't afraid. So they led me back down the ramp and over to Jerry. He was still hauling back on the restraints the men had on him. I called to him, 'Jerry, Jerry, come on, it isn't too bad. It sure didn't hurt me any.' Jerry's eyes were glassed over and he was foaming from sweat, so I called out to him again.

"Finally he replied to me, 'Jerry? Jerry who? He left... he isn't here right now.'

"I wanted to laugh, but I felt sorry for him. I had never seen him lose it like that. He was really scared of that train. I went over close to him and told him I would walk right beside him and help him climb the ramp. This felt sort of strange to me, cause usually I was the one that needed Jerry to help me not to be afraid, and here I was helping him to get it under control. It made me feel good that I could return the favor and help him out this time. He started to follow me, but the closer he got to the train and the ramp, the harder he shook. When we put one foot on the ramp, he realized he just couldn't do it. He reared and almost fell over backwards. Then he spun and threw Bill up against me. Bill went 'OOOOfffff!' and kind of crumpled to the ground in a heap. By the time Bill could jump to his feet, Jerry had pulled the other guys half a block. Bill ran and helped the other two men stop Jerry. Slowly they got him to edge his way up by me. I tried again to reassure him. I wanted so bad to help my friend, but I didn't know how. Then Bill took his hankie out of his pocket. He talked softly to Jerry and patted him, to quiet him down, slowly they wrapped the hankie around Jerry's eyes. As soon as he couldn't see that horrible train he calmed right down.

"Then Bill said to me, 'Okay Tex, you have got to help Jerry. I want you to walk along side him and let him lean on you, so we can get him up on to this boxcar.'

"I did just what he asked. I walked real slow but didn't stop when I hit the ramp. I just kept walking and telling Jerry he was okay. Surprise! We made it up on to that boxcar without anymore outburst from Jerry. After they got us on and securely tied. Bill removed the hankie. Jerry refused to open his eyes. Poor Jerry's knees were shaking so bad that they made a knocking noise that matched the clanging of the train engine."

The young horses interrupted me, as they all chimed in together. "Who would be afraid of a train? None of us are."

"Well kids, you need to remember, Jerry and I were true country horses. This city stuff was real new to both of us. Trains were something we had never seen and they were even new to the area." They accepted my explanation and I went on with my story.

"Bill came up between us and just kept talking to us in his gentle soft voice. I was still a little nervous. Poor old traumatized Jerry wanted to just lay down and die, so he could escape the terror he was feeling. The train blew its whistle and spit out a mountain size puff of steam. It made a hard jolt that threw us all back a little. Remember, Jerry wouldn't open his eyes, no sir, not for me or anyone else for that matter. He just wasn't going to look, even when the train started to move."

I couldn't help myself, thinking back made me start to laugh, Chester joined in. Tipper and the others looked at us with a funny stare. "What's so funny Tex?" Tipper asked, as she started to catch our giggle.

"When the train started to move and it jolted us back we had to take a small step forward to get ourselves positioned again. The train started out very slowly and with a rocking sort of motion. So Jerry thought he couldn't be moving unless his legs were going up and down, so he proceeded to start to walk in place. He lifted his feet high and slowly, just like he was in a parade or something. His prancing hooves made a dull thumping sound on the box car floor. It sounded like a drummer keeping time to some sort of music. At first he kept in perfect time to the speed of the train. I asked him what he was doing and he practically shouted at me, 'Tex... get going, or you will be left behind.'

By this time our giggles turned into roars of laughter. I was trying to stop laughing, so I could tell the story. I was laughing so hard that I snorted and oats flew out of my nose. I had tears running down my face.

"Well Tex, for pete sakes," Tipper said, laughing along with us.

Pretty soon everyone in the barn was laughing and not really understanding what they were laughing about. I continued my story as I laughed.

"That was bad enough, but as the train went faster so did Jerry's feet. I tried to tell him he didn't need to do that, but he wouldn't believe me. I said, 'Jerry, open your eyes. Look, the whole thing is moving, not just us. If you try to keep this pace up you will die for sure by the time we get to where we are going!' The whole barn got caught up in my story and the walls were ringing in laughter.

"Wait; wait it gets even better," I roared. "Just as Jerry was walking in place as fast as he could go, we came up onto a tunnel. And of course Jerry picked that moment to open his eyes. All he saw was a big black hole coming towards him. He let out a very loud grunt and I saw his body start to crumble.

"I must say, I was not too wild about going into that dark hole in the mountain either. But I was so wrapped up in watching Jerry and trying to get him to quit his running in place, that I didn't really think anymore about the tunnel or my own fears. Poor Jerry, on the other hand, had reached his breaking point. I think he was about ready to faint. As we started into the tunnel he did stop running, but only to fall to his knees and put his head down between his legs.

"Bill couldn't contain himself any longer, he started to laugh at him. He got to laughing so hard that he popped his suspenders right off. When we reached daylight at the other end of the tunnel, I saw Bill holding his pants up with one hand, and trying to get Jerry back up to his feet with his other hand. It was a sight to behold."

The laughter in the barn had reached its peak and everyone was snorting and blowing. All the commotion caused the dust to fall down from the rafters.

I pulled myself together and started to continue the story, when Tipper said, "I bet Jerry would just kill you if he knew you told us about him and the train. He seems like such a proud fire horse"

I finished my laughter and said, "You got that right Tipper." I took a deep breath and went on. "Jerry finally came to the realization that he would still be moving even though his feet were still. Bill and I stopped laughing at him, and we all settled down and started to really enjoy the ride." The barn and all the laughter quieted as I continued.

"The cool air blowing on us felt good and it was neat to get someplace and not have to be the one getting us there. As we went through the canyon we enjoyed the scenery. The mountains and the rivers were a beautiful sight to see. There were deer down at the river getting drinks of cold fresh water. They looked so peaceful and content. We saw beaver dams and otters swimming in the river; eagles were swooping down to catch their breakfast, even an old moose was browsing in the shallows of the river. Watching the river flow past with its steady rolling motion made us feel content and sleepy. I think both of us, and Bill, caught a little nap. But all of that was disturbed when we heard the train whistle screaming again. Jerry jumped but held fast. We both were starting to understand this new and wonderful adventure we were on. We were enjoying the ride, but it seemed to end too soon. We reached the Belton depot and were unloaded without any incidents. But I must confess I think Jerry was mighty pleased to be standing on ground that wasn't moving."

Chapter 7:
The Accident

"Remember, I told you that Bill was an exciting sort of fellow, well he was, and boy did he like money. He wasn't afraid to take chances in order to make it, and he wanted lots of it. So he used us in anyway possible to achieve his goals.

"Well, that man that came and hired Bill and us, was not an honest sort of joker. He was as crooked as they come. He was running around the valley telling everyone that there was oil in the mountains up the North Fork River. This con artist was selling stock to unsuspecting good folks. He was telling them all that he could make them rich.. But he needed some money up front to get the materials to build the derricks needed to drill for the oil. He suckered our good man Bill into the scheme along with all the rest of the innocent people he had hoodwinked. He told Bill that if he would use his teams to take the derricks up the river towards Kintla Lake, to the spots he wanted to start drilling, he would give him free stock in the wells. Well good old Bill, being a very honest up front sort of a guy, thought what a deal. He thought everyone was honest like himself. He thought that with no money out of his pocket, and a chance to get rich, it would be a real good deal. Little did he know, that it would be a total disaster for him and almost death for us.

"He took the job with all the enthusiasm of a kid going to the ice cream parlor. When we started out on this new adventure, it was the hardest work we had ever faced. The trails were not even trails. They were real rough, almost impassable! We had to fight our way through the brush and fallen trees. A couple of men went ahead of us and chopped a way through, but we had to pull the wagons up and over the stuff they were falling to build the trail.

"By the time we started on this job it was late summer and everything was dry and brittle. Every step we took snapped and popped. The twigs under our feet would crackle just like breaking glass. As time went on, and the more we traveled over the trail, the better it got for us. I couldn't tell you how many trips we made from Belton to the first derrick location, but we were getting so used to the terrain and the trail that Bill would lay on the goods and take a nap and just let us take him back and forth up and down that trail. We knew our job and he knew he could trust us with his life. We were all doing quite well.

"Fall was fast on its way now, and our trail was worn down and in pretty good shape. The dew at night made things moist and softened the trail. The surest sign for us that fall was coming was that the nights were starting to get colder. The trees were also a dead give away. They were showing us the change of the season from summer to fall, by changing to all their beautiful colors of orange, red and yellow. It would also freeze a little at night now, and that helped the trees to complete their change. The bright new colors were a welcomed sight.

"With the leaves falling off of the trees; it opened up the forest so we could see through it better. Without all the undergrowth and leaves on everything our vision was opened to a much wider area. We also got to see and learn things about trees that we had not known before. Like in the area where we were working, there was a lot of these very unique fir trees they called Larch-Fir, or Tamarack. It is unique to its species because it's the only fir tree that sheds its needles in the fall like a leaf tree. Its needles turn yellow and gold and when the wind blows a little they fall off of the tree. They float gently to the ground like snowflakes do. As we pulled the wagons and felt the gentle warm fall breezes in our hair, the needles fell down around us and made us feel like we were walking in a place that was magical. It seemed as if it was snowing beautiful gold from the sky. The sun shining through the trees made the needles shimmer, and we pretended to be in a fairytale land. We pretended to round a corner and come onto something like a Unicorn or a flying Pegasus. It truly was a magical place with the trail coated with gold fur needles, so we pretended we were walking on a street paved with gold. All of our day dreaming made our job of drudge and hard work a little easier to bear. The men weren't too happy with the needles though, because they do tend to get into everything. But we thought they were pretty."

Tipper had to add her two cents worth, "I should have been there because a horse of my grace and beauty should always travel down a road of gold."

I just ignored her comment and went on talking. "For some reason we always felt fresher and stronger in the fall. Our work felt easier. I guess it was the crispness and the coolness to the air. As this pleasant time to work went on, the men started to get weird on us. They would take instant breaks from pulling and setting the derricks up, every time they heard an elk bugle. A "bugle" means to talk in elk talk. The males bugle to scare away other males and to let the girls know they are in town. We grew to love that sound, because on some days, we got to stand around and eat all day. Those goofy old men would chase the elusive elk all day and into the evening until dark."

"Have any of you kids ever got to see an elk?" I asked.

"I have." Tipper said, in a smart tone of voice.

" So have I," a little voice from the back chimed in.

"They are really something to see aren't they?" I replied.

The little voice from the back said, "The first time I saw one it scared me real bad, because of those big antlers they have."

"Yeah," Tipper said, butting in, "The way they curl down around their heads is really amazing."

"Around their heads," I answered in bewilderment. "Elk have antlers not horns, they don't curl down around their heads, and they stick up into the air from the tops of their heads. Tipper, you must be thinking that a mountain sheep is an elk."

"What!" she snapped.

We all started laughing, because you just never could catch Tipper being wrong about anything. She would tell you that herself.

"Let me explain what they look like, just for you Tipper." I said laughingly. She flipped around and turned her back to me and immediately stuck up her tail. "They are very majestic looking animals, Tipper. The kings of forest you might say. They have wisdom about the forest and they can survive just about anything that comes their way, from bad winters to persistent hunters. They are kind of shaped like us horses, they have beautiful golden bodies with dark hair around their neck and heads. In the fall though, their body color turns grayer so they blend in with their surroundings. The girls, or cows as the man calls them, have no antlers, but boy, do they have big ears. The boys or bulls have these huge antlers that stick up by their ears. You can tell how old they are by counting how many points they have on their antlers. Kind of like counting our teeth."

"Oh, okay!" Tipper snapped again, "I think I get the picture. I know what they look like now. You know Tex, I really don't care about the wild life out there anyway. I want to know about the scary stuff that happened to you and Jerry. That is... if it really happened," she said in her better-than-you tone of voice.

I think she was trying to get back at me for showing her to be wrong about something. I just love ruffling her feathers.

Just then out of the dark came a large dark red horse that said in a low deep strong voice. "Oh it all happened all right. I know because I saw it with my own eyes. I was one of the first to carry hay and oats up to Tex and Jerry. You're right Tex; these kids have a lot to learn. They don't have a clue about tough times or struggling to stay alive. Or even what it means to be a true friend for that matter. Go on with your story Tex. I'll sit on this little sassy one if necessary." The sternness of his voice echoed in the dark, still barn.

"That won't be necessary sir," Tipper said in a very meek little voice. "Go ahead Tex, finish your story."

The rest of the young horses were as quiet as mice.

"Well let's just forget about those elusive elk. But they do have a part in my story later.

"As the fall progressed, we could feel a sense of urgency on the part of Bill and the other men. They wanted to have something to show all the investors so they would be happy and give more money. We overheard the men saying that they hoped they could get one more derrick up before the big snowstorms hit. So we figured that we would be making one last haul up the river. It was snowing now and then, but winter seemed to be starting out pretty mild, it looked to be what the men called an open winter. Here it was December and we were still able to go back into the North Fork country, which was notorious for a lot of snow and bad weather.

"We had a hunch that Bill was getting ready for another trip. Because when ever we were going to make a trip he would feed us a lot more. He would check our feet, the harnesses and the wagons. Sometimes he would stay up all night working on the harness or the wagon. We kind of liked it when he did that, because he always gave us another leaf of hay on his way back to the house. We really didn't understand all this ritual, but I am sure it paid off for him in the long run.

"The men stopped by the barn and were telling Bill that night that they wanted to get one more job done before Christmas. Well, the next day was December twentieth and we still had hardly any snow and weather was unusually warm. We had a very pleasant trip on the train up to Belton.

"After unloading from the train at Belton and starting up the trail we kind of figured it had to be the last trip of the year for us up the North Fork. As we traveled north, the weather started to change and get very cold, but it was still a very clear day. With a load this heavy, we were breathing hard right off the get-go. The steam from our nostrils floated back towards the men on the wagon. As the hills got a little steeper and pulling them got a little harder, you could hardly see anything behind us because we were breathing so hard and making so much steam. Our bodies got hot and started to sweat, that added to the cloudy fume floating up off of us. The load was awkward and heavy, so after we had covered a few miles, Bill shouted out and said that we could use a hand. They brought up another team to hook up with us. We looked them over and thought... 'oh well... let's see if they can really be of any help to us.' We didn't know this team at all; they belonged to another man that was working up there with us. We didn't like working with other teams very much, especially ones we didn't know, but in this case with this kind of load we were grateful to have the help, or so we thought. The man that owned the other team insisted that they be hooked closest to the wagon. We weren't sure if that was the best thing to do, but we knew we needed some help. So we went along with whatever that man said. Bill was nervous, but also wanted to give us some help.

"We were getting farther north and starting to get into the snow. The snow on the trail started getting a little deeper; the wagon was bogging down on us and we had to pull almost as hard as we did during the competitions. The trail was a steady climb, but now we were faced with a mountain, or at least that is what it looked like to us. This was going to be a big hill to pull, so Bill stopped us to let us rest awhile. He sent some men ahead to walk up the road and check things out. Because of winter and the freezing and thawing of the ground, the roads would fall apart and get real rutty and rough. The big rocks got frozen hard into the ground, and the men could barely get them to break loose in order to move them out of our way. They wanted to check out the hill and the road to see if there was anything that would stop us from making it to the top. After a short time they came back and said it looked pretty good, except right at the top. It had a big rut that could make the wagon lean down hill pretty bad. Bill said, 'oh, I think I can keep the team up high and stay up above that one. Let's give it a try anyway.'

"The other team was unseasoned and because they had never pulled with us before, they were getting anxious. They started stomping and pulling at their bits. They were pushing on us and making us a little agitated. All of their impatience made us think we needed to get going sooner than we were really ready to.

"Bill signaled us to 'get up!' And with a flick of the reins we started our climb up the steep hill. Like I said, the hill was steep, real steep, and the snow was getting deeper. The other team didn't know how to gage themselves on this sort of pull. They would lunge and jump and pull in uneven strides. That pushed us and therefore made our strides uneven also. They didn't work together in perfect timing like we normally did. They were trying to pull the hill in one big surge forward. We knew better than that, but also knew that we had to do our share of pulling. So we gave in and surged with them. Our timing was off and so were our strides, it caused us to not have very much pulling power. Even though it was a fiasco, we just about made it to the top.

"All of a sudden with one big groan the other team ran plumb out of gas. That left it up to the two of us to try to desperately hold the wagon, the load and them. They were just giving up on us. We squatted deep and dug in, we strained and pulled and tried our best. But try as we might, we were unable to hold the big heavy wagon and the other team. We started to slide backwards; our feet were grasping for some dry strong ground. Bill was shouting encouragement to us. He was slapping the other team with the rains to try to give us some help. Jerry and I were thinking, oh man; we are in the middle of one of a horse's biggest nightmares. So the two of us dug in even deeper into the half-frozen ground. We lunged forward again to try to get the wagon and load steady and going back up hill instead of down. The other team was still absolutely no help; they were not pulling at all, even with the efforts from Bill. Finally, with big groans and grunts; we started to move the wagon back up hill again. Our legs were burning in pain and every muscle in our bodies was giving all they had to give. The burn was unbelievable and our feet felt like they were going to leave our bodies. The road was narrow and it was starting to get slick from us digging in with our feet.

"We were in the process of making one last lurch forward when we could feel the load shifting on us. It started to slide over into the big rut the men had told Bill about. At that point, it seemed like our movements and time had switched suddenly to slow motion. The wagon slid a little, it hit the rut, and then gently started to turn over on its side over the bank. We were in a total panic now, thinking we were about to fall off the edge with the whole load. But in an instant, the load just popped off, and went tumbling down the hill. As soon as we felt the load go, the wagon got lighter, and started to right itself back onto the road. Jerry and I seized that opportunity and took one last huge jump up the hill. We managed to save the wagon and the other team. They had started to slide off of the bank when we made our big surge forward. I guess they might have caught some footing, and helped us out just a little, but it didn't seem to me like they had done much of anything.

"When we reached a safe spot at the top of the hill Bill stopped us. He pulled us up and jumped down. Our hearts felt like they wanted to jump right out of our chests. They were beating so hard that our breast collars were jumping up and down like they were on springs. We were breathing so hard that we couldn't even hear Bill talking to us. He came up to us and patted and praised us for a job well done. He hugged us and kissed our noses and told us we were wonder horses. He had a large adrenaline rush going, but so did we. The sweat was running down the backs of our legs in streams that were flowing as full and as fast as the river was running below us. Our muscles had turned to mush; they were shaking like a dog scratching flees. Our legs and hooves ached with shooting stabbing pain. Our thoughts towards the other team were bad. We wanted to just plain push them off the bank along with the load. Remember when I said we were glad to have their help. Well boy, was I wrong. They almost got us killed! Bill would have never put us in that position or tried to pull that hill if it had just been the two of us pulling, or even if he had known what a worthless team they were.

Bill went running over to the other men. He started babbling like a brook telling them, 'Did you ever see such a thing? I mean to tell you, this is the best darn team in the world! I would have never believed that they could have saved us like that!' Frankly... neither did we!

"The other men said, 'Now Bill settle down, we know your team is good, but we have a problem here, we lost a load.' About that time the guy that was running the show said, 'Oh what the heck, this place is as good a place as any. Let's just set this stuff up here. This is the farthest north we have ever been anyway, so this will work just fine.'

"Tex, Tex, oh Tex, please stop for a minute," Tipper wailed, "I can't breath. That is the scariest thing I have ever heard."

I sighed and said, " Well Tipper, it is going to get even scarier... so you better hold tight to your tail."

The colts were getting as close to Tipper as they could. I had to smile to myself because telling it is fun, but living it was darn scary. I continued to fill them in on what happened next.

"Bill looked relieved to hear that this spot was good enough and boy we sure were glad to hear those words. We knew we couldn't do all the work alone, and that other team was worthless in our point of view. While we were standing there resting, things seemed to be changing. The sky was changing, from its beautiful blue to a dark shade of gray, and it felt sort of warm out. Bill said, 'It feels like a storm coming in. When it is warm like this it usually means snow... and a lot of it. We probably shouldn't hang around here too much longer. If it gets bad we won't be able to make it out of here.'

"The other men knew exactly what Bill was talking about. They all agreed that maybe they better call it a day and just leave the stuff from the wagon where it lay. We needed to get back to Belton and let the storm blow over. We thought, 'heck, maybe this is our last work day up here till spring.' They covered the stuff from the wagon with branches and marked the road real well so they could find it later.

"We were finally getting settled back down and could breathe normal when Bill came back over to us at the wagon. While he was checking us over and making sure the harness was right, he noticed that Jerry had blood running down his leg mixed in with the sweat. He had gotten cut under his forearm where he had caught a branch when we were trying to make it up the hill. Jerry was on the down hill side so he had to scramble even harder than I did. A tree branch must have been sticking out and it cut his side pretty good. Bill used his hankie and water canteen to clean out Jerry's wound. It was pretty deep and Bill looked a little worried about it. Jerry was still running on adrenalin so he didn't seem bothered by it too much. Bill doctored Jerry as best as he could there and reassured him that when we got back to Belton he would fix him up right.

"We all got turned around and started back down that awful hill. Yeah, you guessed it, we had to hold the wagon back pretty much all by ourselves, again that team let us down. By this time we were not at all happy with those two. I told Jerry, 'Now is when we could use Madeline and Carol! They at least had big hearts and I don't think they would have let us down like this team has!'

"About the time we got a good stride going it started to snow. And let me tell you... boy did it ever snow! All the men that were riding horses with us took off. As they passed us, they yelled back at Bill. 'We will wait for you in Belton, so hurry. We'll keep a hot drink for you.' Bill said, "Yeah... sure you will.'

"The snow started to get heavier and the flakes seemed like they were the size of dollars. We made it back into Belton in record time. Even though we had to drag that no good team along with us. When we reached Belton we expected to see the train, but it wasn't there. Bill got to the depot and asked what was up. The depot man told him that the train had gotten stuck in some deep snow up in the pass and would not be coming from the east. He told Bill that he didn't know when it would get there. It might be days. He understood that we were going to get one heck of a snowstorm. Bill knew he could not stay and wait for the train. He had to get home to take care of all his stock and his farm. The man he had taking care of things was sched- uled to leave the next day. Bill figured he could get back that night even though it would be late. He would just have to take care of things late.

"He then asked the depot man if the rest of the crew was around. The man told Bill that they had decided to go ahead and ride out through the canyon road, instead of waiting for a train that wasn't going to come. Bill was not at all surprised to hear that they couldn't bother to wait for him. They were all young, single guys that didn't want to miss even one night at the bar. Bill parked the wagon and unhooked us all. He scrounged up some food and fed us. He checked Jerry's wound and put more grease on it. He figured he would have to rest at the depot for the night and maybe by some chance the train would make it after all. He worried about his place, but just made up his mind that things would be fine, even if he was a day late getting back.

"At dawn, when the train failed to show up, Bill came and fed us and started to get us ready for the long haul home. The long night had been so very cold and the snow had pilled high onto our backs. We were stiff and cold and our muscles felt like they had frozen solid during the night. Jerry's side was starting to hurt pretty bad and it was making him feel sort of sick. When Bill started to lead him over to the wagon he winched in pain. Bill stopped him and said, 'Jerry my ole friend, you and Tex are going to get to have a free walk home. I am going to tie the two of you to the back of the wagon so you don't have to have a harness rubbing on that cut of yours. That other team will just have to pull the wagon out of here.'

"We could feel Bills anxiety and the fact that he was anxious to get home. So were we, for that matter. We pretended to be warmed up and ready to go for Bills sake."

Chapter 8:
Getting Lost,
The Winter of 1900-1901

"We left Belton rather reluctantly, because we had never traveled that route before. We had always ridden the train up and back. I don't know if the other team was familiar with the trail, but most likely they were, that is why Bill probably thought it would be okay to risk going that way. We totally trusted Bill though, and knew he would know the way, or at least be able to figure it out.

"When we started out it was already starting to snow. The flakes seemed even bigger than the day before. We had only covered a few miles when we found ourselves in a full-blown blizzard. In this country they are called white outs. We couldn't even see Bill, and he was just five feet in front of us on the wagon. We were too far from Belton to turn around and I know Bill was getting worried. We could tell Bill was even getting scared, by the way he was making us all move out at a faster pace than normal. He probably was thinking that if he could get down into the valley it might just be raining there instead of snowing. The elevation up in the canyon is just enough higher to get snow when it is raining in the valley. Bill was really pushing the other team and we had no choice but to keep up or be dragged along behind.

"Jerry was trying to stay strong even though his side was starting to hurt real bad. It is at times like this that us horses wish we could talk, cause' I would have said to Bill, 'Please... we have to slow down; Jerry is hurting and having a real hard time keeping up.'

"We continued on, at what seemed to be a racehorse pace. The snow just kept coming, it was pelting us in the face and stinging with every step we took. The wind was so cold that it seemed our breath was freezing as soon as it came out. Our eyelashes were getting so much snow built up on them that our eyes were having a hard time focusing, let alone see through the down pour of snow. We couldn't see Bill and I know he couldn't see us.

"I think Bill got a little lost. And we were, definitely confused. We had no idea where we were when we came to a river. We now know that that river is called the South Fork River. Back then we had never been in that part of the country, nor had we ever crossed that river before. We were pretty far from any area we were familiar with and that made me shiver, cause' I was not sure where we were going. Horses don't like the helpless feeling of being lost and not knowing which way is home.

"The snow was getting deep, so deep and so fast that Bill went completely out of character, he went charging into the river full blast, team, wagon and then us. As soon as I hit the water I became instantly mad at Bill, I was quite upset with him and looked over to complain about him to Jerry.

"Oh my gosh... Jerry had suddenly disappeared! I wanted to scream for help but there wasn't enough time. He had stepped into a very deep hole in the river, and disappeared from site. Where I was crossing it was passable, but where he was crossing there was a drop off, it was a bottomless pit. In a split second he was under the water and I was in a panic! Remember, he was the rock of our team he always held me up. What was I to do? I couldn't think or breathe or do anything!"

I heard gasps come from the crowd of young horses and Tipper acted like she didn't want to hear such stuff. I liked the fact that my story was giving the crowd a thrill and something to think about. So I kicked into high gear to tell them the rest of the river story.

"I only had seconds," I said in a desperate voice, "to make a decision. I remembered my ability to untie ropes and I had watched Bill tie us to the wagon. In a split second I had my rope and then Jerry's rope untied from the wagon. I kept Jerry's rope in my teeth and let mine fall into the river. I was in a full-blown panic... Jerry was floundering and flopping around in the water. First I could see his head, then I couldn't. I was so scared.

"I put a death grip on his rope with my teeth and decided to just start pulling with all my strength. I pulled and he would get closer to me, then he would disappear again. I pulled again and again and finally after what felt like an eternity he got his footing. He jumped towards me and almost knocked me down. He was gasping and choking and trying to keep his balance. I held his lead rope as tight as I could in my teeth until he was finally steady on his feet. My heart was pounding so hard and fast I thought it would just blow up. I felt like it was leaping up and out my throat. I had no idea a heart could beat so hard and keep going. I was struggling to catch my breath when I realized that poor old Jerry could only make gasping sounds, but I heard his 'thank you' loud and clear. We gasped and coughed together and finally caught a normal breath. Our adrenalin was keeping us sharp and making us strong. I think we could have changed the course of that river, if we would have had a lariat on it; we had so much adrenaline pumping through our veins.

"We looked up and across the river on both sides, we couldn't see Bill or the wagon anywhere. We couldn't even tell which way he had gone because the snow was coming down so thick and hard. The snowflakes were the size of silver dollars, and stacking up fast. The wind was blowing and making it hard to keep our eyes open. White outs can make you feel so helpless, because you don't really know which way to turn to be heading in the right direction. You are pretty blind when you are in one."

I stopped telling my story for a second to catch my breath, because even though it is just a story now, I still lived it, and when I tell it I still get as exhausted as I did that awful day. I glanced over at Tipper and thought to myself, 'I hope she doesn't faint from not breathing.'

The barn was real quiet. For a minute or two Tipper wasn't breathing and she couldn't even talk. I honestly thought I would never see Tipper unable to talk. Then out of the silence I heard this gasping, blurting sound. Tipper finally got her breath and shouted, "then what happened?"

"Well... Jerry and I stood there for a minute and tried to figure out which way to go. We went ahead and climbed out of the river. But we didn't know if we were still headed towards home or if we were pointed in the direction we had just come from. We were realizing we were definitely lost. We couldn't find a trail or a track or anything.

"Exhaustion was starting to set in. Our bodies were hot when we hit the water and now the water was starting to freeze on us. I told Jerry, 'Come on, we need to roll in the snow and try to dry ourselves off as much as we can!' I was rolling when I noticed Jerry was just lying there. I got to my feet and went over to urge him to try to roll.

"He answered me with... 'I can't, I just can't... Tex. You better go on without me. I don't think I can move.'

"I got real mad at him and shouted above the roar of the wind, 'friends don't leave friends to die. We are going to get out of this, together, I promise you.' I urged him some more and finally he got up to his feet.

"We started to slowly walk in the direction we thought we needed to go. The snow kept piling up around us. Before we knew it, we were walking in snow that was up to our bellies. I think we must have walked at least five miles or more. I told Jerry we needed to find shelter some place. He was a walking zombie by now, so he didn't even answer me. At that point I knew it was up to me to get us some shelter, but I was scared cause I didn't know how long I could keep Jerry moving, or how far he could go. All I knew was that we needed some kind of shelter, because out here, in the wind and snow, we would die by morning for sure.

"It was getting colder and colder and now it was dark. The wind and snow whipped around us in a threatening, horrifying way. We were walking side by side now, leaning on each other when we needed to. We were staggering and stumbling along. We both took a step in unison and found ourselves down in a creek, luckily we landed on our feet. Jerry couldn't lift his legs high enough to get up and out on the bank on the other side. So we started stumbling up the middle of the creek. The rocks were torture on our feet and legs. They were slick and sharp, but we stumbled on. We had just walked for a few minutes when we came upon a bunch of fir trees with huge over-hanging branches. They covered a good portion of ground including the creek. It was perfect because it was level with the creek, so Jerry could just step out of the water and on to almost totally dry ground. It looked and felt as good as our barn always had. Jerry took a few steps up away from the creek where he collapsed to the ground. I got myself out of the water and kind of looked around. It looked safe and dry and I thought we could rest there for the night and worry about getting back home in the morning. It was warm out of the wind and I was almost able to see; the snow was falling off of my eyelashes and I could breath easier without the wind beating on me.

"I dragged myself up to Jerry and I could see he was still bleeding from his wound. Beings I am not a man and I didn't have any medicine to fix him, I thought I would just start licking his wound. I licked it until it stopped bleeding. Then I laid my body down as close to Jerry as I could, in hopes that I could keep him warm for the night. I put my head up over his back so that my body would hold in his body's heat as much as possible. We were both shivering so hard that the sound of our chattering teeth would probably have scared away any predator that might have been looking for a free meal. I was exhausted and frightened and wondering what might happen to us. We were very cold and very wet from being dunked in the river. Then the snow had built up on our backs as we were walking. Now it was melting and keeping us pretty darn wet.

"While I was lying there trying not to think about the trouble we were in and how cold I was, I found myself starting to feel a little warmth, it was coming from my heart. I was remembering what Madeline had told me. She had said, 'If she was ever to get lost, she would want me to be the one to be with her, because she knew I was strong and brave.'

"With thoughts of her in my heart and mind I got closer to Jerry and closed my eyes to sleep. Neither one of us moved an inch all night. The snow was still coming down and it was cold and damp. We made it through that first night.

"We were both still alive and it was starting to brighten up a little so we knew it had to be a new day. Jerry got up first to my surprise and went to get a drink of water. He walked very stiff and slow. When he reached the water he shivered at the thought of what almost happened to him the day before.

"He shook and said 'Tex; I have to thank you again for helping me yesterday. If you hadn't been there, I probably would have drowned.

Come on... get up... this water tastes pretty good. I sure wish we had a big old pile of hay lying here though.'

"I put my legs out in front of myself and stretched, it felt pretty good. But when I went to get to my feet I couldn't, I fell back down. I tried again and again my legs crumpled under me. Just then I realized how hard I had worked the day before. I must have pulled some muscles in my back and shoulders when I was pulling on Jerry to help get him out of the water, or maybe when we were trying to pull that awful hill. I didn't know what was causing it, all I knew was, I couldn't get up.

"Now it was Jerry's turn, to encourage me to reach deep down and get myself up. Like I had done for him the day before. I strained and struggled. He wouldn't take no for an answer. He kept coaching and encouraging me until, finally I got to my feet, but boy did I hurt all over. I wasn't sure which part of my body hurt the most; my teeth hurt from pulling on Jerry and even my hair hurt on the rest of my body.

"What a rough two days we had spent! I don't think either one of us would ever want to repeat them, but we were taking notice as to how we would encourage each other when it was needed. Our friendship was cemented together and we appreciated each other to the max.

"We were now turning our attention to the fact that our stomachs thought that our throats had been cut. We found a little dry grass around the area where we were at and along the creek. We ate what we found and believe me it wasn't much.

"While we were standing there, we thought our little house in the forest was pretty neat. It was tall enough for us to stand comfortably in, and we had water right there too. The limbs of the trees were so thick that it was dry under them, which kept us dry and sort of warm. The only thing was, the sun couldn't penetrate the thickness of the tree limbs, so we were kind of in the dark all the time.

"The little bit of food we found was not enough to kill even the smallest hunger pain. While we were listening to our stomachs growl we talked about how we would get out of here. Jerry said, 'Let's just follow the creek, it will lead us to the river and then we can follow the river and find the road we came in on. Then it would only be a matter of following the trail out.'

"I, on the other hand, thought we should stay put and wait for Bill to find us. My argument with Jerry for staying put was, 'what if we think we are going in the right direction and in reality we aren't, and we end up going farther away from home?' Jerry reminded me that we would know which way we were going by the flow of the river. I finally agreed but said, 'You know, Jerry, I am hurting too bad I can't do it today.'

"Jerry agreed, so we spent that whole day just sleeping and lying around resting. The snow didn't let up and we were finding ourselves being buried alive under the trees. We were safe enough, but we couldn't get out, because the snow had gotten too deep, and it had shut off all of the routes out. Even the creek that flowed out from under the trees where we were was snowed in too deep for us to walk down it. Bill couldn't have found us even if he tried. We were completely shut off from the outside world.

"I don't know how many days and nights passed, but we just remained in our little cave. We would talk about when we were kids and try to keep things light and happy. Other wise we would have gone crazy. Everyday we would try to get out, but the snow was merciless, it would not let up or melt. As the days crept by we were starting to lose hope that anyone would ever find us. One day Jerry would try to cheer me up and the next day I would try to cheer him up. I know if I had been alone up there and didn't have Jerry for support, I would have died right off. He told me he felt the same way after we were rescued. Having each other to lean on and a friend to talk to helped keep the darkness in our cave at bay. It would have been too scary to be in the dark alone day after day. We kept wondering exactly how many days had gone by but couldn't be sure because no real sunlight was getting in.

"Some days a little moss would float down the creek and we would get a nibble of food, but most days we were eating sticks off of the bushes. I would pretend that they were wonderful green blades of grass. I would laugh and ask Jerry, 'isn't this the best clover you have ever tasted?' He would go along with me and say, 'yeah, I wish we had friends to share it with.'

Tipper said in a soft sincere voice. "I think I am starting to understand what it means to be a true friend to someone."

"Well good, Tipper. I am glad my long story is teaching you a little something. It sure taught Jerry and me a lot."

Chapter 9:
The Search

"Back in town there was a lot of going's-on that we didn't know anything about. One thing was, that Bill was trying to get a few guys together to help him come look for us. Apparently after he had crossed the river, he never bothered to look back to see if we were still coming along behind him, so he didn't know that we were gone. I think that even if he had looked back he would not have been able to tell if we were there or not. The snow was coming down so heavy and hard that he could hardly see ahead of himself, let alone behind. It was so cold that all he was thinking about was wrapping his scarf a little tighter around his face to protect himself from the blowing snowstorm. I am sure he only had strong thoughts about hurrying and getting back to town, and maybe getting that hot drink the other men had promised him when he got back. Darkness was threatening to set in also and trap him and the other team for sure. I would be willing to bet that he was afraid for his life as well, because there was no shelter anywhere along the way.

"Back in town the men he had worked with were having small twinges of guilt. With the snow coming down so hard a couple of the guys started to feel real guilty and thought that they had better ride back out and see if they could help Bill find his way through the canyon.

"When they reached Bill the storm was starting to settle down a little; at least you could see a few feet away from yourself again. The first thing they asked him was, 'where in the heck are Tex and Jerry.' Needless to say when he finally looked back and discovered we were gone, he was so upset he didn't know what to do. He had come too far and he was just too darn cold to want to stop, turn around and go back to try to find us. So one of the guys volunteered to ride back up the road a little and see if he could see any sign of us. When he got back, he told Bill there was no sign of us, the snow had covered all signs of tracks, and even Bills wagon tracks were totally gone. Bill knew he had to make a decision and make it quick. He knew the other team wasn't us and he knew he couldn't expect as much from them.. They were shivering cold and were so exhausted from trying to pull the wagon through the now very deep snow. They decided to just unhitch the team and Bill would ride out on one of them. The men helped him to put the wagon in a safe place, where they knew they could come back and get it after the storm had gone. The snow was getting too deep for everyone, especially a team trying to pull a wagon. He knew if they didn't get going they would freeze for sure and would not be able to save anything or anyone. He had no choice but to keep heading for town. He just couldn't afford to lose someone else's team; after all, it looked like he had already lost the best team he ever had. He was also thinking about the fact that there was no one at his house that night to keep a fire burning and to take care of all his other animals.

"He had full confidence in us though, and thought we would be able to follow his tracks out. The story is, that he sat at home all night and stayed awake watching to see if we would make it back home. The next day when we didn't show up, Bill started trying to get some guys to help find us. A few guys volunteered, but made it real clear to Bill that they were only prepared to spend a day or two looking for us. Bill was happy for any help he could get. I think he really liked us and after we had saved the day I think the other men respected us also.

"As soon as the snow stopped coming down in buckets, the men went out to see if they could pick up our trail. Well of course, they couldn't, because there was no trail left, we had walked up along the side of the river until we fell into the creek. Then we walked up the middle of the creek to our little house under the trees. So the snow had covered any trail that was left, including Bills. He couldn't even find where he had crossed the river. The men were on snowshoes so they could at least get around in the deep snow. We, on the other hand, couldn't leave our house at all. The snow was just too deep to even try to get out. If, by some chance, they had made it as far up the river as we had they wouldn't have seen us anyway, because of the way the tree limbs where buried in the snow around us. It seemed as if we would be lost forever!

"Christmas came and went and Bill was just sick at not being able to find us. He went out every day trying to figure out which way we had gone and where we could be. He had to go by snowshoe, so couldn't cover a lot of ground, but he made himself a system and just kept at it day and night.

"Now it was New Years Eve and Bill made a toast to the New Year and to us. He made a New Year resolution that he was going to find us, alive, and before the month was up.

"New Years day was bitter and cold outside and inside. The coldness wasn't just from the bad weather. Bad things were to come into play in Bills life. The news was spreading like wildfire. The so-called big fancy oilman was a rip off artist. He took his get-rich-quick schemes and left town by the cover of darkness, never to be heard from again. Also taking a great deal of money from all the good people he had swindled. Bill was sick because he had left a good paying job to do all of that man's hauling. The guy had promised to pay Bill for all his hard work and for losing us. Bill was expecting to get some money that very next week from him. He had told Bill that he would pay him for half his work with stock in the wells, and half with cash. Bill needed the cash pretty bad, his credit was extended about as far as it could go and he had no cash left in the bank. Things were looking real bad for our good man Bill. He was starting to get real worried about how he would make it until spring with no money. He knew come spring he would have ways of making money again, but right now the situation looked pretty bleak.

"After Bill heard the bad news and it had sunk in good and deep, he became obsessed with finding us. He needed us real bad now, because we were such a good team. He could at least sell us or trade us for enough to make it through the rest of the winter. He also wasn't going to let that awful man be the reason we died. He was focused and sure he could find us in time. He knew though, that our time was running short and that the bad weather was not helping things. Bill understood horses real well and he knew that we couldn't survive very long without food or water. He also understood our thinking so that made him even surer that he could figure out where we were. He knew we were people horses, so he figured we would not want to stay out in the wilderness any longer than necessary. He was sure that if he made himself think like we did, he could definitely figure out which way we went and where we were.

"Every day, no matter what the weather was like, Bill went looking for us. But, always to his sorrow, he would go home without even seeing a trace. But his heart just kept telling him we were still alive and he knew he couldn't give up. Every morning he would wake up with a new promise that if he looked hard enough he could and would find us. All I can say is we were sure grateful that he never gave up on us."

The silence in the barn was broken when I heard what sounded like someone crying. I looked over to see Tipper being very upset.

"I don't think I want to hear anymore Tex," she whimpered. "This is the saddest and scariest story I have ever heard and that poor man Bill, what was he to do?"

"Cheer up Tipper, it has a happy ending, cause I am here telling it, aren't I?" I said calmly, to reassure her.

"Oh yes," she kind of laughed at herself, "of course..... I guess I was just really getting into the story. Please go on and tell us something good, Ok?"

"Ok... well remember... it was January now and January is famous for its January thaws. The warm chinook winds blew into the area. You all know what chinook winds are don't you?"

Tipper said, "This one I do know for sure. The chinook winds are a warm wind that blows in from the southwest. They are wonderful because they melt the snow and warm our bones."

"That's right Tipper, good girl, I knew you weren't a hopeless blonde, HA HA HA."

"Ok Tex, that is enough of that, finish your story. I am dying to know where and how Bill found you," Tipper answered, but not in her sassy voice. She was either getting very tired or she was learning something.

Chapter 10:
A Struggle to Survive

"While all this was going on in town, Jerry and I were still struggling on a daily basis to survive. Tipper... I feel I must warn you this is the scariest part of my story, so prepare yourself little girl."

She pulled one of the younger horses close to her and put her head up and over his back. The young horse looked up at her and said, "Look, we are just like Tex and Jerry, we are giving each other support and making each other feel safe. Does this mean we are friends Tipper?"

I expected her to retort sharply back at him but instead she said in a full-grown womanly soft voice, "Yes it does."

I said, "Well here we go, and here is the rest of my story. We didn't have anything of any value to eat. We ate anything we could find in our little house. Remember, the limbs where buried in the snow so we were trapped under the tree. We found some old huckleberry plants that had a few berries on them and some June berry bushes. We ate dead leaves and dug in the creek for what little bits of moss we could find. Having the water there though really saved us, because if we would have had to live on eating snow, I know we wouldn't have made it. We were getting to the point that we just wanted to lay down and go to sleep permanently. We were so hungry and our bony bodies couldn't keep us warm anymore, no matter how hard we shook throughout the nights.

"The January thaw was hard at work and we didn't even realize it, until this one morning after what I thought was the longest, worst night we had spent so far. It had been what seemed to be the coldest of all, and we were getting so weak. I opened my eyes and to my amazement, I thought that it seemed brighter in our dark little house. When I leaned forward to get up I realized that sun was hitting me in the face and it felt wonderful and warm. Our freezing flesh was actually warming up a little. I looked up and to my surprise, saw out and into the daylight. The thaw had melted the snow in the creek enough to let the beautiful sun come in.

"Even though I was feeling the fear that we wouldn't live another day, I couldn't help but notice the beauty of that particular morning. Maybe it was seeing sun for the first time in a long time, or maybe it was the fact that I had just lived through another night, I don't exactly know. All I do know for sure, is that when I looked out, it was beautiful. There was frost in the air everywhere. The sun turned the ice crystals into a million small diamonds. They were floating ever so gently from the sky, looking for a place to land their delicate little selves on. The branches of the trees seemed to be reaching out with welcoming arms to greet each sparkling crystals, offering themselves as a strong silent place for them to perch. They landed and then welcomed the next crystals to join them. Each crystal had its own unique shape and size. They were so delicate, their shapes were so perfect and each one was different. They look like lace from a lady's dress, I was mesmerized by their beauty and I just laid there staring at them. The sun shining through them gave each one the colors of the rainbow. They were turning the trees into shining, shimmering gifts, of brilliance. As I just kept watching them in awe of their beauty, my mind drifted off and I thought again of Madeline and the warmth of her next to me. I imagined the two of us under her favorite tree. I pretended that all the crystals were hanging from it all around us, making it more special to us than any other place in the world. I could see her big dark eyes in the sparkle of every tree branch and wondered if she was warm and safe, and did she ever think of me. I let my thoughts believe that she did and that if she could, she would be right here beside me, keeping me warm.

"My dream world was rudely shattered by Jerry leaping to his feet and saying, 'Tex, the snow has melted enough for us to get out of here... let's go!'

"By this time we had scraped and dug and even stripped the trees of some of their bark to try to stay alive. We knew we had to try to get out and find some desperately needed food.

"We stopped for a minute and looked at each other in the sunlight. It sent ice-cold chills down our spines. Our eyes were sunken and our bodies were just bones with skin hanging on them. We could count every rib on each others bodies. Our hip bones stuck out and when we moved they looked like they would break. We could see the big holes in our manes where our hair had fallen out. We had eaten that hair along with the dead leaves and needles that were on the floor of our snow prison.

"I need to warn you young horses about a very important fact. You see, we horses can't live very long without a steady diet of some kind of food. It takes a lot of food to make the amount of energy it takes to keep our big bodies going. Jerry and I came to the chilling reality that we did not have to much longer to live if we didn't find some kind of food, and fast.

"We touched each other's faces to reassure ourselves. The fear we were feeling was real evident in our sunken eyes. We both told each other how scared we were, but we had to be strong and help each other make it out of this snowy cold place.

"We took deep breaths and set out down the creek to try to reach the river so we could find some food. Jerry led the way in his bold and brave way. Even though he was nothing but a rack of bones he still carried himself with pride and strength. We took one painful step at a time, the pain in our bones was tremendous but we just couldn't stop. The closer we got to the river the warmer the sun felt on us. We had not felt the sun for what felt like an eternity. When we finally stumbled out onto the riverbed we were greeted with a nice surprise. There at our feet were small tuffs of grass that had grown between the rocks. The water from the river had dropped some to reveal it to us. It was the only place that the snow wasn't up to our bellies. We ate like wild men and before we knew it, it was all gone. We stopped and looked at each other and laughed. As we stood there our minds started to clear and we knew what we had to do. We had to follow the river down stream and pray that someone would find us before we had another freezing blizzard that would surely kill us. It was very hard walking on the rocks and we still had our lead ropes on our halters. We kept stepping on them and they would make us fall and scrape ourselves on the rocks. We stopped and looked at each other. I said, 'Jerry... I can't believe we never thought of this before. Here... you eat my rope and I will eat yours.' You know they didn't taste half-bad."

Tipper gagged and said, "Oh Tex, that grosses me out! How could you?"

"You know, Tipper, this story would be real boring if it wasn't for you and your sound affects." I said to her.

We all laughed... and they all listened as I went on with my story.

"Anyway, after we ate the ropes we had a little burst of energy and it helped us go farther on down the river. We just kept saying, 'one step at a time, take one step at a time, we can do this.' Listening to each other's voices helped to encourage us to keep going. We also kept telling each other if Bill were here he would be telling us that we are a wonder team and that if anyone can do it, we can.

"Dusk was setting in and we were starting to get scared, how would we survive without our little house. We knew we needed to find shelter before it got dark and the air got cold again.

"Remember... I said that the elk would come back into the story?"

"Yes I remember," Tipper yelled in a very excited voice.

"Settle down Tipper." I replied. But there was no calming her or stopping her.

"No, no don't tell us, I just can't hear about it! I know it will be too scary for us and too awful to hear. I just know this can't be good. They are too big and too scary... I just know that they did something horrible to you! They are spooky creatures, I just know it! My mom always said to stay clear of them; that the forest belonged to them and that they would protect it at all costs!" Then she leaned over and pulled the young horse even closer to herself.

"Oh Tipper you sweet thing," I chuckled at her.... "I guess I need to teach you a little something about them. The truth is, your mom meant well, but apparently she had never had any personal contact with any elk. You need not worry. Forget all you have heard about them and learn from what I teach you right here and now. The truth is, they didn't hurt us or anything, in fact it was the contrary. As we were stumbling down the river we came onto a small herd of them and they proceeded to come right up to us. At first we were kind of scared and were thinking just like you are right now, but they moved slowly and didn't offer any sort of threat. They walked quietly up to us and reached out their noses in a gesture of friendship, we touched noses with them. Then they motioned for us to follow them. We thought, 'what the heck! We have nothing to lose. Without shelter we would surely die tonight.' They led us down the river a little farther and they brought us to a small lake. It was frozen, and as we crossed it we noticed that the bank on the other side had a southern exposure. The January thaw had melted large amounts of snow off the hillside. The thaw had opened a lot of bare spots that had grass and bushes to eat. We could hardly contain our joy.

"The elk then showed us where the creek was coming out of the lake. It was running and wasn't frozen. We got a nice drink and then went to the hillside to eat. We ate so fast and furious that we both ended up with cramps in our stomachs. We were starting to double over in pain, when the elk motioned for us to follow them again. We knew we had to stop eating, so we willingly followed them.

"As the darkness was falling the elk led us to a large overhanging fir tree. We crawled under and lay down to rest. To our surprise the elk laid down around us. The warmth from their bodies renewed us and felt like warm summer sun. We told each other good night and drifted off to sleep.

"We woke up with a jolt from the sounds we were hearing. When we were in the snow cave, it was totally quiet, so every little sound now sounded extra big to us. This sound we were hearing all of a sudden sounded like a rifle going off. I jumped with every bang. Jerry leaned over and said to me. 'Tex, that noise you are hearing is the sap in the trees getting frozen. When that happens the trees make that cracking noise.'

'Oh, I remember now... I guess I am just a little spooked. After all here we lay with wild animals out in a wilderness. I never thought this would happen to us.'

"It did feel good though, to be able to look up and see the stars. They were brilliant and looked like they were close enough to touch. It was a full moon and a totally clear, cold night. The moon made it almost as bright as day and it gave everything a beautiful glow. I thought, 'if only Madeline was here. We used to stay awake all night on nights like these counting stars.'

"Jerry and I started to talk, and we made up our minds that we would just stay here with the elk, where there was a little food and water. Besides, the snow was way too deep through the woods to try to make it out. We also did not know where we were. The snow made the forest look so different and we couldn't smell where the men had gone. We just had to believe that Bill would find us. We knew that we were not like the elk and that we couldn't survive on such little amounts of food.

"A few days passed and the food was disappearing fast; there were a lot of us eating it. The elk were going farther away from us everyday and we were sure that our days were coming to a definite end.

"One day the elk were real nervous and acting like they could see and smell something they didn't like. So we followed them into the woods to see just what was making them so nervous. As we were struggling to get through the deep snow we noticed something that we recognized, snowshoe prints. We leaned down and could pick up a faint smell of our friend Bill. We got so excited that we started to whinny and stomp around in hopes he would hear us and see our footprints."

A very loud scream broke the intensity of the story. I jumped about a foot off the ground!

"My goodness Tipper, what is your problem?" I yelled at the young filly, "You scared me half to death!"

She was still screaming but not quite so loudly now. "You guys, it is a mouse," She squealed, "It is walking on the rail of Tex's stall, right here under my nose!"

"Oh for pete's sake Tipper, it isn't going to hurt you and it will only eat a few of our oats anyway!" I told her, in a disgusted voice.

She realized how foolish she was being, so she calmed herself down and continued in a squeaky voice, "Please, please tell us they found you. I don't think I can stand another moment of wondering if you were rescued or not"

I laughed very loud and said, "How soon we forget, or is it that you are really getting lost in my story. Tipper, aren't I here, and am I not telling this story?"

Her face was glowing red in the dim light of the barn. She laughed a little and said, "Yeah... you're right, it is you telling the story about yourself, and you are here, and you are ok. I did it again, I keep forgetting this story is about you.. please go on Tex." The old horses were now starting to go to sleep. But the young horses were still in awe and wondering, how did those elk know we needed help?

"Ok now, back to the rest of the story, and back to Bill and the elk. You know to this day I wonder myself... how did those elk know that we needed help?

"We were too weak to follow Bill's tracks through the deep snow. So, very slowly we worked our way back to the hillside and the lesser snow. We hoped that with every breath we took that Bill would come back and find us. Our walk might have been a mistake because we had just used up what little energy we had built up with the small amounts of food we had been eating.

"We could only find one little tuft of grass left, it was frozen solid and the dirt stayed stuck to the end of it. We shared it, receiving one small bite each. It was so cold that all it did was add to our misery; we could feel it go down and into our stomachs one frozen inch at a time. It caused our stomachs to ache and wrench. Our legs became so weak that we both fell to the ground in a heap. We were almost delirious now, and we couldn't get any part of our bodies to move. We wanted desperately to at least get back to the over hanging trees but neither of us could budge.

"The wind was starting to blow and the snow started to fall slowly at first and then it proceeded to turn into a real dumping. It started to cover our broken bodies. I looked over to see my dear friend Jerry being completely covered over with snow. His head was disappearing as I watched. I tried to reach out to him, but couldn't get my head to even move an inch. I drifted off into a semi-conscious state and dreamt of being back in my younger days as a colt. I was loping along with the breeze in my face. I was in a green and luscious pasture of waist high grasses. The sun was bright and so... very... warm, I felt like I was free. I felt no pain, and I was floating away like on a cloud. I began to feel warm all over. 'If this is the end, it feels pretty good,' I thought. I was starting to give into the fact that maybe I was going to freeze to death.

"All of a sudden, something snapped me out of my dream. I looked up and much to my surprise, there in front of me rearing up and shouting at me was my one and only true love, Madeline. She was shining like a star, but her voice was sharp and stern.

"She shouted, 'Tex, get up, get up right now! Get up to your feet! Go wake up Jerry, Tex! do you hear me? You can not lie here, not even for one more minute! Listen to me. You must be the brave strong horse I know you are. Get up and follow me. RIGHT NOW!'

"Then like a floating angel she turned and began to gallop off into the direction of the snowshoe tracks. Her words burned into my brain. The sound of her voice made my muscles come to life. Her melodic sound gave my whole being a surge of strength. I struggled to my feet; I took one step then buckled to my knees. I struggled up again as I heard her voice push me on. I wobbled, staggered and drug myself over to where Jerry was laying, now buried in the snow. He was just a mound of white, so still that I was afraid Madeline's pleas were too late. I reached down and brushed away the snow from his face the best I could with my nose. I reached down again and searched out his face for his halter. I prayed that I could get a good grip on it and pull hard enough that I could maybe bring some life into what seemed to be his lifeless body. My fears were mounting as I found and grasped the leather strap. I pulled on it. It was so big on him from all the weight he had lost. It lifted what seemed to be a foot before it felt tight. I pulled and begged him with my weak voice to try to get up. I pulled again and he didn't even budge. 'Oh no! Was I too late? Is he gone?' I asked myself.

"MADELINE! MADELINE!' I cried out, hoping to hear her voice again, reassuring me that everything would be okay. My mind was starting to race; please, I couldn't be left out here alone. So I did all I knew how to do and all I could do. I pulled on Jerry's halter as hard as I could; I pulled again and again. Finally, as his snow-filled face emerged from the snow bank, he opened his eyes and asked, 'Are we in heaven yet?'

"I told him in a very shaky weak voice, 'No, but you must get to your feet. If you stay lying here it will be the end of you for sure!' I pulled hard on his head again. He lifted his head and tried to pull his legs out in front of himself so he could get up. He couldn't get them to budge. I took my foot and put it behind his leg and pulled it towards me. We worked together and managed to get both legs out in front of him. He made it to a sitting position but couldn't rock himself up. At that moment I felt so alone. I was having shock waves of fear. A sweet gentle voice came to me again, 'don't give up Tex, try again.'

"I got behind Jerry and pushed against him with the last ounce of strength I could muster. His boney body creaked and cracked and I feared that his bones would break from the pressure of me pushing on him. He let out a loud grunt and lifted himself to his feet. We were both staggering and swaying back and forth and doing all we could to try to walk towards the snowshoe prints. We were walking in a stupor, and probably in circles, but we kept thinking if we could just keep moving we would not freeze. We felt like we were truly dead, but had just forgotten to lie down."

Chapter 11:
The Rescue

"We were at our weakest, lowest point, when we heard off in the distance a familiar sound. A warm friendly voice we had enjoyed hearing every morning for the last few years.

"Dawn was breaking and through the mist we could faintly see the figure of a man walking towards us. Then we heard the wonderful sound of his voice again. It was like music to our ears and at first we were kind of scared and not sure if what we were hearing and seeing was real.

"Well boys... it is about time I found you, and look at the two of you, sleep walking on the job. I told you, you are my 'wonder team.' I knew you wouldn't let me down. I knew you would make it.'

"Was he real or were we just seeing a mirage? Could he just be an angel or was it truly our friend Bill? At this point in time our minds were so dull we did not know the difference. We wanted it to be him; we needed it to be him. He spoke again; we whimpered a whinny, and wanted to leap with joy to the sound of his wonderful voice, but all we could do is lift our heads up from dragging along on the ground. We had just survived the worst night of our lives.

"We thought we had been alone all night, but the elk had stayed close to us. When they heard Bill's voice they got scared. His voice didn't bring them any joy like it did us. They ran off into the forest to escape the human that they feared so much.

"Bill had tears running down his face and he kept kissing us and stroking us and telling us how sorry he was that he had lost us. He helped us get back to the shelter and the over hanging limbs. There, he put blankets on us from his bedroll. He rubbed our bodies and generated some warmth to our carcasses. He built a huge fire that gave the first true warmth to our broken, scrawny bodies. He heated some water and put a hand full of oats in it. He fed us one small bite at a time. When the warmth from the oats hit our stomachs it felt like a nice warm wood stove. I will never forget how it brought life back into my almost lost body. He gave us a flake of hay that he had packed in and said he would be back in the morning with more food. We didn't want to see him leave, but we were too weak to stage a protest. We knew we could trust him and if he said he would be back, then darn it, he would be back."

I had to stop talking and compose myself. Big tears were running down my face. I know I made it and I know we both are okay to this day, but I still have a hard time talking about almost dying.

The whole barn was sobbing and being strangely quiet. Tipper was leaning against me and getting me soaking wet from her tears. I took a deep breath and let out a loud sigh so I could continue the rest of my story.

"The next day he came back at the crack of dawn with two bales of hay and a big bag of oats. Our good friend Pete over there was the one that carried all of it into us."

Pete spoke up in his very deep voice, "Yeah, it wasn't easy wading through that deep snow with those heavy ole things on my back either."

"Yeah, Yeah Pete, I have paid you back at least a dozen times for that." I said as I grinned at him.

"I know Tex, but I just can't let you get too comfortable now, can I?" as he returned the grin.

"Well anyway, our friend Pete there brought us hay and oats. He made that trip every other day for six days. Every night when Bill would leave, the elk would come back and help us clean up the hay. We were slowly, but surely, getting stronger and stronger. Then the day came when Bill said to us, 'well boys, today is the day that we start to get you out of here. After breakfast we are going to get started. Pete will lead the way.' Then Bill said to us, 'boys I don't want what you had to live through to be forgotten, so look what I made back at my wood shop.' He took out this sign he had made and hung it on a tree close to the little lake. It said, " Tex and Jerry's, Hungry Horse Lake." We now know the name stuck.

"The weather was being real good to us, as we were having one Chinook after another. The snow was packing pretty well in spots, where the wind and sun would hit it. But in the trees and the shade we still had to wade through belly deep snow. It was real hard going at times.

"Pete lead the way and we stayed real close behind him. This time we would not get lost, that is for sure. We couldn't walk too fast, and Pete and Bill were real patient with us. They waited and helped us every step of the way.

"Our first night on the trail turned out to be a pretty scary one for Bill though. Remember our elk friends? Well, they were kind of following us because of the food. That night, after Bill fell asleep, our friends came in and shared our hay with us. Then they bedded down just like always.

At dawn when Bill woke up and saw them, he could hardly believe his eyes. He jumped to his feet and ran for his gun. Well in his rush and commotion he scared the heck out of the elk. There were feet, horns, and tails flying everywhere! It was a wonder that Bill didn't get stomped to death. He finally found his gun and started setting it off one shot after another. The three of us stood very wide-eyed, wondering what all the fuss was about. Finally, Bill quit running around, and gasping for air, he told us 'boy I scared them away didn't I? Now boys, you know I would never let anything or anyone hurt you, don't you!' I think it took poor old Bill till about lunchtime to settle down after his big scare from the "killer elk." If only he had known those elk had saved our lives."

The barn was ringing with laughter again and I think all the young horses were getting a real thrill out of my story.

"It took us three days to reach the town of Columbia Falls. We were exhausted and real glad to reach a place that we knew had food and shelter. Winter was far from over and it is very hard to gain weight when it is cold. It takes all the food you eat just to keep you warm, and help your body grow enough hair to protect you from the cold.

"Bill went immediately to the local store, and then the bar and told everyone that he had found his team and they were alive. No one believed him. So he said, 'well, follow me and I will show them to you.' Everyone from town came out to see us. They were in total shock and kept asking Bill if we were the same horses. They would say, they are so skinny, how can they still be alive? How did they make it out of there? We just can't believe it!' Ladies would cry and men would gasp in amazement looking at us. Then one fellow said, 'well all I can say is, that canyon up there is sure Hungry Horse Country.' Bill said, 'you sure got that right. I made a sign, naming the lake where I found them Hungry Horse Lake, and the creek Hungry Horse Creek.'

Tipper chimed in, "And that is how you and Jerry became famous?"

"Yes Tipper, you could say we are famous," I told her... "famous or not I am just glad that I had a friend like Jerry that never gave up, and an owner like Bill, who risked his own life, to save ours."

"How did you end up here then, and how did Jerry end up being a fire horse?" Tipper asked, her voice was so mature that it caught me off guard.

I stammered and said, "Well Tipper, remember how I had told you that I was not real graceful and Jerry was."

"Yes." she replied.

"Bill could have lost everything when that man ran out and didn't pay him, so he had to let us go. He gave me to the KM for a bill he owed them because I wasn't the most graceful. He sold Jerry to a fella that was a fireman. He took Jerry to the fire department because he knew how coordinated he was and he knew he could do a good job for them. Bill used that money to keep going until more work came along for him."

"Did that hurt your feelings Tex?" Tipper sympathetically asked.

"No," I replied, "I am a horse and I have to do what the man tells me to do. I did miss Jerry real bad though and it was hard not living on Bills ranch, but I really like my job. And yes I really like my team mate also."

Tipper glowed and swished her tail while she flipped her head and said to the others, "I told you that he liked me." Her beautiful white mane and foretop softly fell over one eye. For a moment I saw Madeline.

The rest of the young horses thanked me and said that they had learned a lot and that they now understood what friendship, courage and a strong will to live meant. The old horses were all snoring. I turned to go back into my stall, when Tipper came up to me and leaned against me.

She said in a soft mature voice, "Maybe someday, you will look at me like you used to look at Madeline."

"Well you never know." I said in a soft voice. I reached over and gave her ear a nibble. She blushed. I went quietly to the back of my stall and wondered, "In the future, would anyone ever know that Jerry and I were famous during our lives?"

Well Tex and Jerry, this author is pleased to tell you, that yes, in the future you will be remembered in a loving way. You also will be remembered forever because at this writing there is not just a little lake named for you, but a big reservoir lake, a creek, a town, a dam, streets, stores, bars, statues, and now this book.

I understand that both Tex and Jerry retired from their jobs and lived to be grand old horses. They also made their marks on our lives and in our hearts.

The End

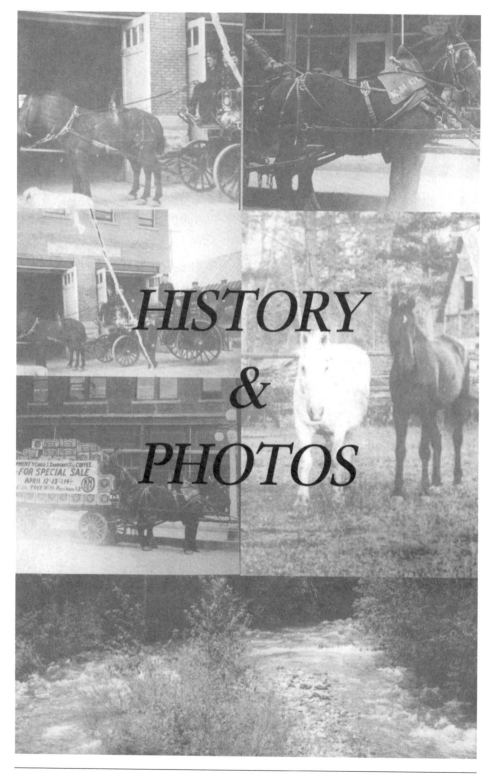

HISTORY
&
PHOTOS

The name first started in 1901 with the discovery of the two freight horses on a small lake with a creek flowing into it. I searched back as far as I could, and the lake and the creek were the first two things named for the horses.

Hungry Horse Creek

Also in 1901 the canyon running up the South Fork River was called Hungry Horse Canyon.

In 1909, the Hungry Horse Ranger Station was established. Back then, it was sometimes just the ranger's house. It was located in the Hungry Horse Canyon area.

In 1924, a surveyor by the name of Paul A. or E. E. Jones, both were named as the man who completed an engineering survey on the area they called Hungry Horse Canyon, which is still in existence today. It can be seen and enjoyed by following the lower dam road along the beautiful South Fork River. His survey was the start of thinking and planning for a dam in this canyon. They had looked other areas over but this one seemed the most likely and best suited for such a project. The reason for a dam was to help with irrigation and water shed control for Flat-

Hungry Horse Canyon

head Valley, which at the time was growing slowly. The possibility of mining and oil was begining to bring in more people and the Great Northern Railroad was opening things up a might. The agriculture needs in the valley were growing and so a dam was a pretty sure thing.

Bureau of Reclamation

In 1943, the Bureau of Reclamation started building an office and some housing for the employees in hopes that Congress would okay a dam. All was wishful thinking on the part of a large number of people.

But in February, 1940, a newspaper man named Harry J. Kelly, chairman of the Kalispell Chamber of Commerce, waged a campaign to get the dam to become a reality. He wrote letters and got everyone he knew to do the same. He was friendly with Mike Mansfield and so he inundated him with reasons why they should build the dam. Of course the people who were getting good jobs from the project backed him one-hundred percent, and so did the local businesses and the business men that had foresight. He became such a nuisance. They nicknamed him Hungry Horse Harry.

In 1943, Mike Mansfield submitted a bill to build the Hungry Horse Dam at a location in the South Fork River, five miles from where it joined the Middle Fork River. In 1944, the senate passed the bill to start the clearing and preparing the dam. On July 10, 1948, they started construction on the dam.

Hungry Horse Bar

MARTIN CITY, MONT.

Downtown Martin City

1946 saw the start of a brand new town that would be named Martin City. This author grew up and raised her son there. The town boomed. In 1946 there were only four businesses, one of them called the Hungry Horse Bar. It cashed worker's pay checks and entertained families. At one time it would close on Sunday mornings so they could have church, and on weekend nights would show movies until the show house was built. The bar was owned by a man named Sally Rand. It had horse foot prints in the cement on the sidewalk leading you in the front door. At least one cowboy every year had to ride his horse up and into the bar and up to the bar inside and and ask for a cold one. Sally would smile and ask, "Do you want one for the horse too? Then he would kindly show him the way out. We kids usually could make a couple of bucks off of those cowboys by taking care of their horses until they sobered up and were ready to go on their way. It was a good thing Sally knew all of us and could send them in the right direction to fetch up their horses.

One year later this small town would boast that it had 53 businesses and that it was the most scenic boomtown in America.

In 1960, the famed bar that was the center of Martin City burned to the ground along with the rest of the block.

HUNGRY HORSES

1946 also saw the start of the Hungry Horse Newspaper. It's first puplication was on August 8th, 1946. The owner/publisher was Mel Ruder. He was a wonderful writer and a talented photographer. During his many years as editor and chief of his paper he won prestigious awards for his photography, and he also won a Pulitzer Prize. As of this writing, he has also been named in the Newspaper Hall of Fame. He wrote about the Hungry Horses

Hungry Horse News

in 1946 and he reprinted the same article in a 1996 paper. This later article is what made me finally sit down and write out the story for this book. Thanks Mel...

Hungry Horse Chapel

Also during the same time Hungry Horse Government Project was growing, businesses were sprouting up all over. There was a small disagreement on how people should conduct them selves, so the now existing townsite was divided into two separate areas: Hungry Horse Project, and an area called South Fork. This area of the South Fork wrote articles to the paper stating that they had a city with no joints, no liquor and no gambling. They had their own grocery store and coffee shops and even some cabins.

The town was brought into Hungry Horse when the Post Office was opened in that area in 1948. They built their church and it was called the Assembly of Columbia Falls. Today, this area has grown to have one of the most beautiful Bible camps in the state and a wonderful church known since 1973 as the Hungry Horse Chapel.

1948 Hungry Horse School

*These original carvings are on display
at the Hungry Horse Corral.*

Hungry Horse Corral

In 1947, Morris Blake, one of Montana's Highway Patrolmen, carved a statue of a very hungry horse to commemorate the construction of the dam. He retired from the Highway Patrol in 1953 due to injuries sustained during the line of duty. In 1955 he opened a wood carving shop and made those hungry horses famous. After his death in 1965, his widow ran the business. In 1982 she sold the business to Vaughn and Irene Shafer. They delight in continuing on his wonderful work at what is called the Hungry Horse Corral.

Hungry Horse 1950

Hungry Horse Project

Hungry Horse Supermarket

1948 was the year that almost everything came together. The project was at its fullest. They built the new school and named it Hungry Horse School. The Post Office was also built and boasted a figure of a hungry horse on it, and had a statue built in its honor. The town was now a real townsite. The residents were so proud of it they made signs that still tell you today that you are entering Hungry Horse, Montana. Also that year a business was built that is now the Hungry Horse Supermarket. In 1948 it was called Home and Contractors Supply, then the Pennywise Pharmacy was added and shared the building. After the dam was done, it stayed just a pharmacy for a few years, but its name was changed around 1970 to the Hungry Horse Pharmacy. Groceries were added and today it is a supermarket.

Hungry Horse Fire Starion

The new Hungry Horse Fire Department (all volunteers) built in the mid seventies.

Hungry Horse Post Office

The town was established as Hungry Horse when the Post Office was opened in 1948.

Hungry Horse Motel

In 1950, the Hungry Horse Motel was built. It carries its original name today and the present owners want to keep it's 50's decor and the slower pace of that era.

Hungry Horse Dam

1952 saw the completion of the Hungry Horse Dam. At its completion, it was the third highest and the fourth largest concrete dam in the world. It is 564 ft. high and 2,115 ft. long. The dam created a reservoir called the Hungry Horse Reservoir, and it is 34 miles long. It is completely surrounded by national forest and boasts several very nice campgrounds and tons of fishing spots, including Hungry Horse Creek and Bay. While at the bay you have a wonderful sight of Hungry Horse Mountain. There is also a very small lake called Hungry Horse Lake.

Hungry Horse Dam Reservoir

Hungry Horse Dam Overflow

Some tell a tale that Tex and Jerry were found at a small lake that is now the overflow tunnel for the dam. Don't know if this is true, but was told it very well could be.

Hungry Horse Baptist Church

And last but not least, the Hungry Horse Baptist Church named in 1990, formerly called Whities Club Rocco. This establishment had the finest dining within miles and fed and took care of the dam workers. It was told that the carpeting would be nothing but white concrete dust at the end of the night. I personally admired that beautiful carpet because I worked there as a waitress in the 1980's and the carpet still looked brand new after forty years of cork boots and concrete dust.

Hopefully I covered everything that was and is called Hungry Horse. If I left out something or someone I apologize, and I hope that in the future, new things will be named for those two brave horses.

Judy

KM Delivery Horses in the 1900's

Kalispell Fire Department Horses in the 1900's

Thanks
Tex and Jerry